Columbia University
STUDIES IN ENGLISH AND COMPARATIVE LITERATURE

THE ARTISAN IN ELIZABETHAN LITERATURE

THE ARTISAN

IN

ELIZABETHAN LITERATURE

BY

CHARLES W. CAMP

1972

OCTAGON BOOKS

New York

Reprinted 1972

by special arrangement with Columbia University Press

OCTAGON BOOKS

A DIVISION OF FARRAR, STRAUS & GIROUX, INC.

19 Union Square West

New York, N. Y. 10003

LIBRARY OF CONGRESS CATALOG CARD NUMBER: 73-159171

ISBN 0-374-91261-0

Printed in U.S.A. by

NOBLE OFFSET PRINTERS, INC.

NEW YORK 3, N. Y.

J. G. Whittier's *The Shoemakers*

Ho! workers of the old time styled
    The Gentle Craft of Leather!
Young brothers of the ancient guild,
    Stand forth once more together!
Call out again your long array,
    In the olden merry manner!
Once more, on gay St. Crispin's day,
    Fling out your blazoned banner!

Rap, rap! upon the well-worn stone
    How falls the polished hammer!
Rap, rap! the measured sound has grown
    A quick and merry clamor.
Now shape the sole! now deftly curl
    The glossy vamp around it,
And bless the while the bright-eyed girl
    Whose gentle fingers bound it!
. . . .

The foremost still, by day or night,
    On moated mound or heather
Where'er the need of trampled right
    Brought toiling men together;
Where the free burghers from the wall
    Defied the mail-clad master,
Than yours, at Freedom's trumpet-call,
    No craftsmen rallied faster.
. . . .

The red brick to the mason's hand,
    The brown earth to the tiller's,
The shoe in yours shall wealth command,
    Like fairy Cinderella's!
As they who shunned the household maid
    Beheld the crown upon her,
So all shall see your toil repaid
    With hearth and home and honor.

Then let the toast be freely quaffed,
    In water cool and brimming,
"All honor to the good old Craft,
    Its merry men and women!"
Call out again your long array,
    In the old time's pleasant manner:
Once more, on gay St. Crispin's day,
    Fling out his blazoned banner!

PREFACE

Though the subject of the merchant and craft guilds is a favorite one among historical writers, it has not attracted students of literature. However frequently the artisan appears in the poems and plays of the Middle Ages and Elizabethan period, he has not as yet been the subject of study as a literary figure. *Shakespeare's England,* 1916, 2 volumes, though careful in its treatment of the literature and history of the period, has almost nothing to say on this subject. The author, therefore, has made a study of the artisan and his family at work and at play as they appear in English literature during the period, approximately, 1557 to 1642. Consideration is also given to the development of the treatment of artisans, simple and direct in the early period of Elizabeth's reign and imitative and sophisticated in the reigns of James I and Charles I.

This volume does not contain all that the writer has to say on the subject of craftsmen in literature. Further discussion of the subject will soon be ready for publication.

The author is under obligation for stimulus and guidance to Professors A. H. Thorndike, H. M. Ayres, and W. W. Lawrence, all of Columbia University; and for certain suggestions to Professor J. H. Cox of West Virginia University.

CHARLES W. CAMP.

CONTENTS

THE ARTISAN IN ELIZABETHAN
LITERATURE

THE ARTISAN IN ELIZABETHAN LITERATURE

INTRODUCTION

Attention in this essay is devoted to individuals and types rather than to organizations. For a complete understanding of the craftsman or craftswoman, however, brief mention must be made of the medieval and Renaissance guilds.

As may be seen from the bibliography, much has been written on the history of guilds. A few words, therefore, are all that need be said here of the craft guilds. Originating from the beginning of the 11th to the middle of the 13th century, the craft guilds attained their greatest power in the 14th and 15th centuries. Formed for self-defense against barons, they protected themselves not only by co-operation, but also by self-criticism, since defective workmanship or dishonest trading on the part of any members of the guild would injure the reputation of the rest.

In the 14th century the old idea of fraternity gradually died out, and the guilds became powerful commercial and civic organizations. Toward the end of the reign of Edward III were established the following merchant companies, called the twelve great livery companies: mercers, grocers, drapers, fishmongers, goldsmiths, skinners, merchant-tailors, haberdashers,

1

salters, ironmongers, vintners, and cloth-workers. They
are interesting in that the Lord Mayor of London was
chosen from their ranks and in that from their number
several famous capitalists and philanthropists emerged.
These were Simon Eyre, draper, founder of Leadenhall,
Thomas Gresham,[1] builder of the Royal Exchange, and
Richard Whittington, mercer, founder of Whittington
College.

Instances of government interference in affairs of
trade, of some interest and importance, may be studied
in the acts of the Privy Council. A good illustration
is the Statute of Apprentices, 1563. It compelled certain
poor persons to work for arbitrarily assigned wages
termed "reasonable wages." There were restrictions
on the hiring of a man from another parish. Working
hours were regulated so as to gain the best effects of
daylight, night work being forbidden as not conducive
to good workmanship. Technical education was provided for apprentices, and the proportion of these to
journeymen was regulated. Artisans might apprentice
only the sons of freemen; shopkeepers and merchants
might apprentice only the well-to-do.

English apprenticeship probably started in the 13th
century.[2] Toward the end of this century the records
become more numerous. By 1300, London records were
kept of the enrollment of apprentices; in the country
this system was adopted later. It involved a youth's
binding himself to a master craftsman by indenture;
i. e., by contract for a definite term, usually seven years,

[1] Gresham was a mercer, according to The Dictionary of
National Biography, and Hazlitt's *Livery Companies*, p. 182;
he was a grocer, according to Heywood's *If you know not me*.
[2] Dunlop and Denman: *English Apprenticeship and Child
Labor*, p. 18.

with certain agreements. In the 15th century the recording of the contract was emphasized. There was also a proviso that apprentices must be twenty-four at the end of their term, and must remain single until that time. The length of the term varied: the goldsmiths, inasmuch as their craft involved much dexterity and skill, insisted upon a ten-year period; certain of the lesser trades were satisfied with less than seven years.

A feature of the system which is very important, but sometimes overlooked, is the personal relation between the master and the apprentice, and frequently between the latter and the mistress and fellow-apprentices and journeymen. Not only in the shop, but also in the home and in his private life did the apprentice come under the care and discipline of the master. He was supplied with food, lodging, clothes, and education, not only in the craft, but also, to some extent, in reading and writing. He ate with his fellows at the master's table, was strictly guarded and watched as to his outside amusements, being forbidden, in accordance with the terms of his indenture, to frequent taverns, to play dice or cards, or to be guilty of any incivility.[3] The aim of the system was to furnish a skilled workman and an upright citizen.

The master, in turn, was obliged to clothe, feed, and instruct the apprentice in the proper manner, or he was liable to be fined.[4] (Guild officers went on rounds of inspection, a supervision which became especially prominent in the 16th century.) The master had a

---

[3] Dunlop, p. 55.

[4] A master was fined for improperly clothing his apprentice. Clode: *History of the Guild of the Merchant-Taylors*, p. 521.

legal right to punish, within certain limits, a wayward apprentice.[5] Apprentices could be discharged for
damages. If the latter amounted to over forty shillings,
and the apprentice was over eighteen, he was considered a criminal. Runaway apprentices were sought
in different towns as if they were fugitive slaves.
On the apprentice's being captured and returned, the
master was authorized to bind him with chains.[6] The
well-behaved apprentice, however, was not considered
a bondman, nor did his position extinguish his right
to be regarded as one of the gentry.[7]

Indeed, well-to-do parents often apprenticed their
sons to one of the more dignified companies, that they
might profit by the discipline and training rather than
by the knowledge of the technique of the particular
craft. The position of apprentice in the mercer's company, e. g., was more dignified than in any other company; such an apprentice did not have to supply his
master with water from a tankard, as did other apprentices. Thus it is that the four royal born youths
in Heywood's *Four Prentices of London* are apprenticed to a mercer, grocer, goldsmith, and haberdasher,
all worshipful companies. Whittington, not poor as the
popular tradition would have us believe, was of well-
to-do parents and apprenticed to a mercer.

In the Middle Ages and the Renaissance, apprenticeship was one of several avenues to citizenship.
Freedom of the town was hereditary. One could become a burgess by gift, purchase, marriage, or by

[5] In the 15th century the Merchant-Taylor Guild fined a man
for unlawfully bruising his apprentice. Clode, p. 510.

[6] R. Brodsky: *Das Lehrlingswesen in England*, p. 28.

[7] Strype: *Complete History of England*, vol. 2, pp. 435-6.

serving as an apprentice to a freeman. If he was not the eldest son of a freeman, he would probably have to serve an apprenticeship to become free.[8]

The 16th century, however, introduced certain changes. Skill was no longer regarded as a requisite for admittance to a guild (the freedom of which also implied freedom of the town) ; but admittance other than by apprenticeship was exceptional.[9] By 1560, qualifications for apprentices, such as birth (apprentices must be of English blood), class, age, education, property, and physique, were stressed. Apprentices were generally forbidden to do any trading, but the Newcastle adventurers allowed them to bargain with limited stock after five years of service. The turning over of apprentices to another master was also restricted in the 16th century. The Statute of Apprentices transformed apprenticeship from a guild system to a national one. A chief aim was to produce English goods of a high order. This statute extended the compulsory seven years' apprenticeship of the woolen industry to all the trades. Sufficient labor was further insured by the poor law of 1601 which compelled parents having too many children to apprentice some of them.

The attire of apprentices was plain. At the end of the 16th century they were compelled to wear blue gowns in winter, and blue coats down to their calves in summer. Flat cloth caps, shining shoes, and plain stockings completed the attire. Apprentices were strictly forbidden to wear silk; they were allowed to carry no weapons except a pocket-knife. Apprentices, however, sometimes wore decorative apparel, as several

[8] Dunlop, p. 40.   [9] Dunlop, p. 50.

prohibitory statutes show; e. g., an ordinance of the mayor, 1582, restricting the gay clothes of apprentices.

The results of such a system of education and discipline were fairly favorable. The apprentice was not overworked; he sometimes had spending money; and he enjoyed many holidays. In his adolescent stage, he was better off in a position of mild servitude than were many unguarded youths of a later period. He came to have a feeling of responsibility as a citizen, without, however, much knowledge of how to show it. Several apprentices often became a mob, and were especially rowdyish in Tudor times. They were involved in such uprisings as Evil May Day, 1517.[10] When any event occurred which did not meet with their approval, the nearby apprentices would cry, "clubs," which was a signal to all apprentices in the neighborhood to arm themselves with cudgels from the shops, and to decide the matter by force. Their energies were boisterous, but seldom well directed.[11] An achievement in which apprentices prided themselves was the destruction of bawds' houses on Shrove Tuesday. The noise and carnage did not end there, however; the ostensible purpose furnished an excuse for wrecking even comparatively innocent establishments.

In literature the apprentice occupies a somewhat conspicuous position when compared with that of

[10] In order to prevent a repetition of the Southwark disorder, the authorities were especially watchful of apprentices on Midsummer Night, 1592. They were to be kept by their masters indoors; theaters and other meeting places were to be closed. *Acts of the Privy Council,* vol. 22, p. 549.

[11] The Roman plays of Shakespeare vividly portray the blind but brutish violence of the lower classes.

journeyman, craftsmaster, or mistress. Authors show such bad aspects of the apprentice as have just been commented on. But they also tend to glorify him, especially in the late 16th century. It is not the mature and experienced journeyman or master that is usually chosen for the subject of a heroic story, but it is the youthful apprentice.

After the seven years' term of service, the apprentice became free, and worked as journeyman for independent masters and for daily wages. In the 15th century the rule became stricter against employing for journeymen any but apprenticed men. In the Middle Ages, journeymen formed guilds, "yeomen guilds," and occasionally rose in revolt against the master craftsmen.[12] At first these associations amounted to little, but by the time of Elizabeth and James they were recognized by the municipality. Journeymen at these later times often married and ceased to wander. Their associations differed from those of the old master craftsmen mainly in being smaller: they had no chance to deal directly with the consumer.[13] Conditions were hard for them; they usually had to work in suburbs and to set up there on opening shops for themselves.[14] Their goal was to become independent masters, but industry and ability were frequently unrewarded. In the 16th century it became increasingly difficult to become a member of a guild; those already members tended to exclude any but their immediate relatives.

There was often required of a candidate for admittance to a guild (a requisite stressed in the 17th cen-

[12] Lipson: *Introduction to Economic History of England*, p. 361.
[13] Lipson, p. 362.   [14] Besant, p. 219.

tury) a masterpiece which embodied original craftsmanship of his particular trade. When this was not
required, a test of some kind was usually called for. If
the work therein was defective, the candidate might
be taken as a hireman (at unsteady pay) in the trade,
or be taken to perform in that craft certain functions
in which he was efficient.[15] Test work was first used
in the tailor's craft, one of the first to become capi-
talistic.[16] If this testing was carried on reasonably and
fairly, it was an efficient standard of admittance; but
impossible requirements in test-work might be made
by those who were determined to exclude a candidate.
Hence the condition of journeymen did not necessarily
imply any lack of dexterity. Greene's *Defense of Connycatching*, e. g.,[17] presents a journeyman tailor more
skilled in his profession than any of the master tailors
in the neighborhood.

The journeyman has a rather inconspicuous place in
English literature with such few exceptions as are to
be found in Deloney's, Dekker's and Rowley's work.

Something has already been said about the master-
craftsman in his relation to the apprentice and journeyman, his necessary qualifications as a teacher and
householder. It now remains to consider him as an
individual. In the Middle Ages, the master-craftsman
was considered fairly respectable and dignified, but he
came to be gradually superseded by the merchant. In
order to prevent this extinction, the more enterprising
ones, such as Simon Eyre, became themselves merchants
by speculating whenever possible; or by being trans-

---

[15] Dunlop, p. 220.
[16] Unwin: *Industrial Organization*, p. 47.
[17] Grosart: *Greene*, vol. 11, p. 87.

ferred from a handicraft to one of the twelve merchant companies. They aspired to become more than mere shopkeepers; they aimed at becoming merchants on a large scale, as Shakespeare's Antonio or Heywood's Gresham. Thereafter it was their ambition to become aldermen, mayors, and perhaps knights. The Lord Mayor of London was elected from one of the twelve companies, but local mayors were often members of smaller guilds.[18]

We have thus far spoken of the boy as an apprentice. Girls also were apprenticed to craftsmasters and mistresses, although rarely.[19] Women might become independent mistresses of a craft, but this also was rare. As early as the 14th century there were cases of girls being apprenticed. But few of those apprenticed, either then or in the late Renaissance, ever became independent mistresses of a craft.[20] The female apprentice was often occupied with helping the craftsman's wife in domestic work rather than with learning a trade. Her father would, in most cases, not pay the expenses (slight though these were) of apprenticing her, but hired her out as a maid of all work. This was much to the disadvantage of a girl; she had long hours and sometimes heavy work, with no such compensating qualities as the male apprentices had who learned one thing well.

Both before and after the Statute of Apprentices, the wives and daughters of craftsmen frequently helped them at their work. A woman who had assisted

[18] In Middleton's *Mayor of Queenborough* Simon the tanner is made **mayor**.

[19] Phillis Flower; e. g., in *The Fair Maid of the Exchange* was a sempstress's apprentice.

[20] Dunlop, p. 153.

her husband at his work for seven years, might, on his decease, take up his trade.[21] Seven years was the minimum term for women as well as for men, according to the Statute of Apprentices.[22] Thus we find women in the silk-weaving, dyeing, sewing, spinning, and brewing crafts. Inasmuch, however, as a woman's time was frequently divided between household duties and the shop, she could seldom hope to become as efficient at a craft as a man who devoted his whole time to it. But her industry and solicitude for her husband's success, as presented in 16th and early 17th century literature often arouse our interest.[23]

Something deserves to be said about the dress of the craftsman's or merchant's wife, since it is associated with her increasing pride in the 17th century, her aspirations toward the courtly class, and her emergence as the social equal of her husband.[24] In 1570 the citizen's wife wore plain but colored clothing and linen caps. But by the 17th century, fashionable ruffs, farthingales, and elaborate aprons appeared. Stubbes, in *The Anatomy of Abuses*, 1583, complains of the number of artificers' wives who wear velvet caps daily, and of the merchants' wives who wear French hoods. Women of these classes also wore exquisite imitation jewels.

After this cursory historical introduction to the crafts in the Middle Ages and Renaissance, brief

[21] Dunlop, p. 143.

[22] One of the poor laws of Elizabeth gave commands to the poor to apprentice their girls until the age of twenty, and the boys until the age of twenty-four.

[23] Deloney's sketch of Eyre's wife or Rowley's Cicely are instances.

[24] This is illustrated in Massinger's *City Madam*, 1632.

attention will now be given to some of the literature of these periods that relates to craftsmen.

The Middle Ages may be hastily surveyed by a consideration of the work of one writer who reflects many phases of medieval literature, Chaucer. In the prologue to his *Canterbury Tales* are a number of artisans, the haberdasher, carpenter, weaver, dyer, upholsterer[25] and wife of Bath (clothworker)[26] being especially substantial, prosperous, and proud. In a number of his tales, moreover; e. g., in the cook's fragmentary story of a riotous apprentice and in the miller's and carpenter's tales there arc good presentations of artisans.

In the 16th century, preceding Elizabeth, literature was both satirical and idealistic. Cheating devices of craftsmen are represented in Skelton's poem, *The*

---

[25] "An Haberdassher and a Carpenter,
A Webbe, a Dyere, and a Tapicer,
Were with us eek, clothed in o liveree,
Of a solempne and greet fraternitee.
Ful fresh and newe hir gere apyked was;*
Hir knyves were y-chaped noght with bras,
But all with silver, wroght ful clene and weel,
Hir girdles and hir pouches every-deel.
Well semed ech of hem a fair burgeys,
To sitten in a yeldhalle on a deys.
Everich, for the wisdom that he can,
Was shaply for to been an alderman.
For catel hadde they y-nogh and rente,
And eek hir wyves wolde it wel assente;
And elles certein were they to blame,
It is ful fair to been y-clept 'ma dame,'
And goon to vigilyes al bifore,
And have a mantel royalliche y-bore."

The Prologue, lines 360-380.

* The privilege of wearing silver instead of brass was reserved for persons of a certain social eminence.

See E. P. Kuhl's *Chaucer's Burgesses* in *Transactions of the Wisconsin Academy of Sciences, Arts, and Letters*, vol. 18.

[26] Chaucer's treatment of the Wife of Bath anticipates Massinger's treatment of the city wife in his *City Madam*.

Tunning of Elynour Rumming, Barclay's *Ship of Fools,
Cocke Lorell's Bote,* and Powell's *Wyll of the Devyll;*
More's *Utopia,* however, translated into English in
1551, contains praise of certain crafts.

In the following chapters representative works from
the time of Queen Elizabeth's coronation to about 1642
will be carefully considered. A certain change in literary attitude is roughly paralleled in all the literary
forms (excepting the Lord Mayor's Show) that we consider: prose, verse (including ballads[27]), and drama.
Time and political vicissitudes alter literary themes:
the Cavalier poetry introduces a different attitude;
Deloney's idealistic writing in the late 16th century
is supplanted by Rowlands' harsh and satiric presentation of artisans in the first two decades of the 17th
century; Dekker's and Rowley's kindly attitude in their
shoemaker plays of the late 16th and early 17th century respectively is supplanted by satire and harsh
realism in the work of later dramatists like Fletcher,
Middleton, and Shirley.

[27] Confusion between the old traditional type of ballad and
the Elizabethan may be obviated by a consideration of the words
of F. B. Gummere:

"On the whole, aside from remoter origins, the ballad under
Elizabeth, so far as it had any literary meaning, evidently
covered on the one hand poems of love or satire which more or
less vaguely suggested the French type, and, on the other, poems
independent of such influence, pointing back to the traditional
ballad, with its refrain, its tune, and its hints of the dance. But
any occasional poem, grave or gay, which appeared as a broadside could take the name unchallenged."

F. B. Gummere's *Old English Ballads,* p. xxiii.

CHAPTER I

THE CRAFTSMAN AS A HEROIC FIGURE

As depicted in the literature under consideration, artisans are extremely fond of spectacular shows, exhibitions, and parades of various kinds. This is well illustrated in the Lord Mayor's Show, a ceremony in which are often represented former patriotic and philanthropic mayors who rose from the craftsmen's ranks.

The novels of Thomas Deloney are rich in heroic craftsmen. In *Jack of Newbury*, the weaver, Jack, brings two hundred and fifty of his own workmen to Queen Katherine to fight against the Scots at Flodden Field.[1] In the same author's *Thomas of Reading*, the clothiers provide King Henry I. with soldiers to fight against Lewis, the French king.

A craft which is best represented in this respect is the so-called Gentle Craft or shoemakers' guild, the popular guild of the late 16th century. In the second part of Deloney's *Gentle Craft*, Stukeley and Strangwidge, sea-captains, visit the shop of Peachy, the shoemaker, and are insolent to the shoemakers, who defend themselves with their tools. Peachy and his men defeat the two sea-captains. It afterwards becomes the custom for two of Peachy's men at a time to whip Stukeley and Strangwidge, so that the latter dread shoemakers and repent their former insolence. The feud is finally

---

[1] *Jack of Newbury*, chap. 20.

settled by the Duke of Suffolk. Peachy, moreover, at
his own cost, arms thirty of his own servants, and
leads them to the king, who needs soldiers to defeat
two thousand Frenchmen who have landed in the Isle
of Wight. Seven of Peachy's men are chosen as the
king's own guard; and Peachy, their captain, is made
the king's shoemaker.

In the prose version (as well as in the play) of
George a Green, the shoemakers of Merry Bradstead
have ordered that all strangers in the town shall trail
their staffs. When Robin Hood and George a Green
and their followers refuse, many shoemakers of the
town come out, armed with cudgels, to compel them
to conform to this old custom. The shoemakers do
not desist from their vigorous fighting until they
recognize George a Green among their opponents.
Robin Hood and George soon fraternize with them,
because of their valor. When George tells them that
he and Robin Hood have traveled from Sherwood
Forest to Bradstead to prove what mettle was in their
fraternity, this is as good as a plaster to every man's
broken head.

More illustrative still of the craftsmen's pride in
their own heroic exploits and intimately associated
with the folk history of the Gentle Craft, are the stories
of Crispine and Crispianus in the first part of Deloney's
Gentle Craft. The stories of Crispine and Crispianus
are warlike, and are based on tradition dear to the
shoemaker's guild. The tyrant, Maximinus, perse-
cutes the sons of the English sovereign, Crispine and
Crispianus. As a refuge, they apprentice themselves
to the shoemakers' trade. Crispine is wooed and won
by the emperor's daughter, Ursula. His brother,

Crispianus, meanwhile, fights bravely against the Persians in France, and defeats the opposing general, Iphicratis. Shoemakers feel greatly flattered on finding that both of these apprentices are of noble blood, and that Crispianus has fought so nobly in battle.

The popularity of these warlike stories is attested by the fact that several plays and chapbooks are based upon them. There is a non-extant play, *Crispin and Crispianus*, acted by the shoemakers' companies of towns before 1643.[2] It was apparently a rough dramatization of Deloney's story. Rowley, in his *Shoemaker a Gentleman*, 1609, dramatizes Deloney's narrative, making a stirring play. Two chapbooks that follow Deloney and that underwent several editions are *The Shoemakers' Glory* and *The History of Crispin and Crispianus*. Crude and improbable though these stories of the Gentle Craft are, they are valuable as illustrations of the craftsmen's pride. They have importance in this study, inasmuch as many of these extravagant tales were believed by credulous craftsmen, especially apprentices, and constantly referred to by them.

Another feature of the works just described is noticeable; i. e., the love of the craftsman for association with royalty. A favorite theme in Deloney's novels is the entertainment of the king by the hero-craftsman. In *Jack of Newbury*, to take an illustration, Jack the weaver is rewarded for his prowess and patriotism by Queen Katharine's "putting forth her lillie white hand and giving it to him to kiss."[3] Another illustration is

[2] Referred to in Halliwell's *Dictionary of Old English Plays*.
[3] Chapter 2.

in the fact that three princes in Deloney's *Gentle Craft* apprentice themselves to shoemakers. Craftsmen, then, were particularly fond of being (if only in the least degree) associated with, or in proximity to royalty, and boasted of any such relation for a long time afterward. A nod or a smile from a king or the enlistment of one of the royal family in one of the great companies was considered an exceptional honor. The artisans themselves often aspire to no less than knighthood and ladyship. This theme occurs frequently in the literature to be discussed. Keen-sighted persons realize that this weakness and susceptibility to flattery exist in craftsmen, and often sway the latter or his family by working on this trait. It is partly for this reason that demagogues like Bolingbroke in *Richard II* and Antony in *Julius Caesar* succeed so well in dealing with craftsmen and citizens, and that Coriolanus, with his inability to flatter, fails so wretchedly. The popular story of Jane Shore is given much tragic force by the fact that she, a goldsmith's wife, is "beloved of a king," and advanced to royal eminence and power, only to be cast down utterly during the period of his successor.

A work, partly prose[4] and partly verse, which extols craftsmen to an extravagant degree is Richard Johnson's *Nine Worthies of London*, 1592, dedicated to Sir William Webbe, Knight and Lord Mayor.[5] It has, for the most part, the favorite theme of the valiant apprentice of low birth, who does deeds of patriotic prowess. Seven of the nine are thus celebrated; the others, Sir Henry Pritchard and especially Sir Thomas White,

---

[4] Prose parts are concerned with dialogues and extravagant eulogies of Clio and Fame; the verse deals with the worthies' accounts of their own histories, and their boasting.

[5] *Harleian Miscellany*, vol. 8.

are celebrated for less spectacular but equally substantial services to the nation. The heroes, with the exception of Sir Thomas White of the period of Queen Mary, are medieval craftsmen like those celebrated in the Lord Mayor Shows, about whom certain popular and frequently erroneous traditions have collected.

The first one, Sir William Walworth, fishmonger and mayor, is an important figure in a study of craftsmen. He is sometimes mentioned as a patriotic model to be followed by soldier craftsmen. As he is famous for his fighting ability and military glory, he is an ever-present figure in the Lord Mayor Shows in which the Mayor-elect is from the ranks of the fishmongers.[6] Walworth is represented as the aged soldier who defeated the rebels of Kent and Essex, stabbing Tyler, the leader of the rebellion. He speaks in high praise of himself, as do all the worthies successively (and as do some of those in the Lord Mayor's Show).

A romantic and patriotic hero of the chivalric period of the Black Prince, the merchant-tailor, Sir John Hawkwood, is very popular. He is celebrated in the Merchant-Tailor Lord Mayor Shows; e. g., in Webster's *Monuments of Honor*. He boastfully describes his conduct in battle as follows:

> That day, the prince of Wales, surnamde 'the Black'
> Did mount me on a gallant English steed;
> Where I bestride me so upon his backe,
> That none incountred me that did not bleed.

---

[6] These spectacular Lord Mayor Shows celebrate exemplary and patriotic mayors of past time; i. e., those valorous in battle and those famous for philanthropy, as White and Pritchard. They differ from Johnson's work, however, in being an equal tribute to the craft itself of the Lord Mayor, and in going into some description of its early history.

This Hawkwood was fourth of the dubbed knights, and was given a gold chain by the Black Prince. He fights for the Duke of Milan, a service for which he gains castles and towers, and helps Spain against the Pope.

Others of the nine who distinguish themselves in a similar way are Sir William Sevenoake, a grocer; Sir John Bonham, a mercer and knight; Sir Christopher Croker, a vintner and knight; and Sir Hugh Caverley, a silk-weaver and knight. This work is clumsy and lacking in force, partly owing to the fact that the heroes boastfully rehearse their own deeds in childish and stereotyped manner. It goes into no detail or differentiation of the various crafts represented; but it illustrates well the interest of the craftsman in shows and spectacles.

Ballads and songs are not deficient in this praise of the valiant artisan. Beginning about 1590 and continuing until about 1605 there are commemorative ballads of patriotic heroism on the part of craftsmen. Perhaps song is the best medium for this; exploits can be better represented thus than on the stage. Of several ballads that enter into extravagant praise of the apprentice as a soldier, *The Honor of a London Prentice*[7] is a good instance. This apprentice defeats twenty Turkish knights in a tournament. Imprisoned with two hungry lions, he thrusts his arms down their throats, tears their hearts out, and throws them at those looking on.

[7] Evans' *Old Ballads*, vol. 3, page 35.
 Seek all the world about,
  And you shall hardly find,
 A man in valour to exceed
  A prentice gallant mind.

Ballads somewhat similar to this one are Deloney's *Shoemakers Song on Crispianus Night;*[8] *A Use of Exhortation to the London Prentices,* 1643;[9] *The Joviol Broom Man;*[10] *How Wat Tyler and Jacke Straw rebelled against King Richard II;*[11] *A Ballad in Praise of London Prentices and what they did at the Cockpit playhouse in Drury Lane,* 1617.[12] Women as well as men from the ranks of the artisans are sometimes the subjects of such ballads, as is the case with Long Meg of Westminster, the stalwart victuallar, subject of a lost ballad written in 1590, ca., *The Coy Cook Maid*[13] portrays an energetic craftswoman who is a match for men. This cook, wrongly called coy, is courted in vain by Irish, Welsh, Spanish and Dutch suitors. She breaks a Scotch suitor's head with her ladle, and threatens to thrust a spit through a French suitor. She is finally won by a poor English tailor. This ballad is interesting partly because of its satire on foreigners.

As was stated before, the popular shoemakers' guild is well celebrated in this respect. Shoemakers are valiant in the prose and dramatic work on George a Green. A shoemaker is a soldier in *Locrine,* 1595, and in Dekker's *Shoemakers' Holiday,* 1599. A play called *Crispin and Crispianus,* acted by the shoemakers' companies of towns before 1643,[14] Rowley's *Shoemaker a*

[8] *The Gentle Craft,* Part 1, end of chap. 9.
[9] Percy Socy. Pub., vol. 1, p. 67.
[10] Roxburghe Ballads, vol. 2, p. 129.
[11] Deloney's *Strange Histories,* Canto 10.
[12] Percy Socy. Pub., vol. 1, p. 94.
[13] Roxburghe Ballad Socy., vol. 3, p. 626.
[14] "Crispin and Crispianus cost more trouble: the princes could ever borrow their tools from any journeyman shoemaker; but then the robes and decorations of the queens and nobles were forced to be carried up and down in knapsacks." *The Original Works of William King, LL. D.,* vol. 1, p. 180.

Gentleman, 1609, and Rawlin's *Rebellion,* 1637,[15] follow
to a greater or less degree Deloney's stories of valiant
shoemakers. In Shakespeare's *Henry V,* 1599, the king
appeals to his fellow-countrymen to fight with him on
the day called "the feast of Crispian."[16] This day,
celebrating the patron saint of the shoemakers, lends a
certain spirit of fraternity and co-operation to Henry's
stirring appeal, reviving in the minds of the artisans
the warlike and chivalric stories of the heroes of the
Gentle Craft.

> We few, we happy few, we band of brothers;
> For he to-day that sheds his blood with me
> Shall be my brother; be he ne'er so vile
> This day shall gentle his condition.[17]

Two plays that deal with popular uprisings of
craftsmen and the repression of these in each case
by a patriotic mayor and craftsmen are Heywood's
Edward IV, Part I, 1600; and the anonymous play,
The Life and Death of Jack Straw, 1593. In the latter,
William Walworth, fishmonger and Lord Mayor, the
stock figure in the fishmonger Lord Mayor's Shows,
gathers patriotic Englishmen and succeeds in quelling
the rebellion and in stabbing Straw, one of the leaders.
According to the play, Walworth's dagger is put in
the city arms by the king.

An interesting play of this nature is Anthony
Brewer's *Love-Sick King,* 1605. Grim the collier of
Newcastle leads an army of his own workmen, and

[15] This play presents tailors as valiant fighters, but follows
roughly the plan of Rowley's *Shoemaker a Gentleman.*

[16] Shakespeare is unhistorical here, the date of the Battle of
Agincourt being unknown.

[17] *Henry V,* Act 4, sc. 3, lines 60-64. "gentle his condition,"
i. e., make him a gentleman.

takes King Canute prisoner. Grim is not in the least
slow in claiming this credit for the Newcastle colliers,
and declares that Newcastle strength has set England
free:

> If you wo'd rake hell and Phlegitan,
> Acaron and Barrathrum, all these
> Low countries cannot yeeld you such a company.
> Tara, ra, ra, ra, ra, O brave master,
> Now for a company of conquering colliers.[18]

For his national service, Grim is made the king's coal-
bearer.

The most famous extant illustration in drama of the
success of craftsmen in battle is Thomas Heywood's
Four Prentices of London, 1594, ca. This, together
with *Bold Beauchamps*, a lost play, dramatizing the
exploits of Thomas, first Earl of Warwick, is referred
to in Beaumont and Fletcher's burlesque, *The Knight
of the Burning Pestle*, 1613. The play has no real
delineation of craftsmen; aside from the fact that we
are told that the Earl of Bouillon's four sons are apprentices to four of the great crafts, they do not refer
to any features of their crafts as Rowley's or Dekker's
craftsmen do to theirs.

The banished earl, disguised as a London citizen,
apprentices his sons as follows: Godfrey, to a mercer;
Guy, to a goldsmith; Charles, to a haberdasher;
Eustace, to a grocer.

> All high born
> Yet of the city-trades they have no scorn.[19]
> . . . .
> Kings themselves have of these trades been free.

[18] A. Brewer: *The Love-Sick King*. A. E. H. Swaen edition,
line 1680. Grim is alluding to the popular association of colliers
with devils.
[19] Page 403. Text is Dodsley: *Old English Plays*, vol. 6.

Guy speaks of the advantage of knowing a trade, inasmuch as all kingdoms are subject to Fortune's frowns; and a banished prince who is skilled in some trade will never want. These princes fight bravely, recover Jerusalem from the infidels, and Guy becomes ruler. Each of the champions bears on his shield the arms of the trade to which he was bound.[20]

The tribute paid to craftsmen as fighters in some of these plays; e. g., *A Shoemaker a Gentleman* or *The Four Prentices of London*, is not as great as it might appear at first sight. In the former play, Crispianus, the prince, is the noble and valiant person (he is shoemaker only as a temporary makeshift) ; Barnaby, the journeyman, is the cowardly churl. In *The Rebellion* we have the noble Giovanni contrasted with the real tailor and coward, Vermine. In Heywood's play these noble youths are craftsmen but for a time. The best tribute to craftsmen is seen in the wishes of Eustace and Charles that they had apprentices from the different towns to help them fight. Certain plays to be considered later, some of which may have been written with those just described in mind, such as *Alarum for London, Coriolanus, The Famous History of the Life and Death of Captain Thomas Stukeley*, as well as such a burlesque as *The Knight of the Burning Pestle*, illustrate the helplessness of untrained citizens in battle. In Beaumont and Fletcher's *Philaster*, for example, the captain exhorts the citizens to leave their

[20] Eustace's grocers' arms on his shield may have suggested to Beaumont and Fletcher to make Ralph a grocer's apprentice in *The Knight of the Burning Pestle.*

A ballad, that is non-extant, perhaps dealing with the same theme, is *The honours achieved in Fraunce and Spaine by four prentices of London,* 1592.

base crafts and shops and to fight nobly; i. e., not in honor of their crafts, but in spite of the fact that they are craftsmen.[21]

[21] Act 5, sc. 1, of *Philaster*. A rather exceptional treatment in the later drama is in Fletcher and Massinger's *The Double Marriage*, after 1622. Here the citizens support Sesse against the tyrant, Ferrand, and make him King of Naples.

CHAPTER II

THE ARTISAN AS SPECULATOR AND PHILANTHROPIST

This chapter represents the craftsmen more as they aspired to be than as they actually were, but it has historical significance, inasmuch as the Elizabethan age was one of speculation. A brief account of the history of the merchant-tailors will illustrate the aspiration of craftsmen from early times through the reign of James I to be considered merchants, a merchant being frequently a master-craftsman as well.[1] The tailors were granted a charter, incorporated a company, and given the name of tailors or linen-armorers by King Edward I. As the company grew, it became a rich and powerful fraternity, taking the function of trading. Henry VII gave the tailors the title of "merchant-tailors," in recognition of their trading privileges. Their pride in the title is shown in *The Merchant-Tailors' Song;* and in Lord Mayor shows that celebrate the election of a mayor who is a tailor, Henry VII is presented among the other kings free of that company, and his charter forming them a trading company is mentioned. Dekker artfully describes the aspiration of craftsmen toward world-wide trade, at the prosperous period of the accession of James I.

"Taylors meant no more to be called merchant-taylors, but

[1] Whether or not a merchant was a master-craftsman, he frequently began as a manual worker, this applying sometimes even to the great merchant-adventurers.

merchants, for their shops were all lead forth in leases to be turned into ships, and with their sheares (instead of a Rudder) would they have cut the Seas (like Leuant Taffaty) and sayld to the West Indies for no worse stuffe to make hose and doublets of, than beaten gold."[2]

The praise of altruistic craftsmen and civic officials from their ranks is to be found in Johnson's *Nine Worthies of London*. White, a merchant-tailor; Pritchard, a vintner and knight; and Sevenoake, a grocer, are instances.

The self-made man is a favorite subject in Deloney's fiction. A brief introduction to this important writer may now be given. He gives a well-rounded delineation of artisans. Himself a silkweaver, Deloney is entirely sympathetic; his very themes are those most pleasing to craftsmen: the rise of the industrious artisan, and especially the exploits of artisans in battle. There is extremely little of the darker aspect of city life, which appears in later literature; i. e., faithlessness within the home, and cheating and bitter rivalry within the shop. Instead, nearly everything is presented in a cheerful atmosphere. There is merry singing accompanying the work (and frequently, which is not the case at present, the songs glorify the work itself), Robin, a journeyman shoemaker, being an especial exponent of this. There is throughout a spirit of fraternity and co-operation. Comic byplots, though often coarse, are humorous, consisting generally of merry pranks. There is a certain amount of romance with the realism, a most successful instance being the love story of Crispine and Ursula. In Deloney's portraits of several energetic, competent, and proud women, he

[2] *The wonderfull yeare*, 1603, Grosart, vol. I, p. 100.

anticipates an interest in, though a different treatment of, the craftsman's wife on the part of several Jacobean writers.

His three novels are *Jack of Newbury*, celebrating weavers; *The Gentle Craft*, in two parts, dealing with shoemakers; and *Thomas of Reading*, celebrating clothiers, — all written between 1596 and 1600. Each novel is a collection of loosely connected stories, usually centering about craftsmen and craftswomen. The stories range from moral ones to coarse farces and horseplay. Taken all in all, there is much charm in the writer; he influenced literature dealing with crafts.

Jack of Newbury, 1596, depicts a historical figure, John Winchcomb, a clothier of the time of Henry VII and Henry VIII, who may have built the church vestry of Newbury. Deloney's treatment follows the main events of Winchcomb's life. He is first presented as an industrious and steady weaver's apprentice, who, at the death of his master, is intrusted by his mistress with the charge of all the workers for three years. She rejects three wealthy suitors, a tanner, tailor, and parson, and woos and weds Jack. Her aggressiveness contrasts with his passiveness, it being a common theme with Deloney to depict a man who is overruled by his wife. On the death of his wife, Jack becomes a rich and eminent clothier, afterwards marrying one of his own poor but industrious servants.

Jack often shows to his servants pictures of great men of humble descent, usually sons of craftsmen. To Jack's workers this serves as an example and an incentive to industry. Some of the pictures are as follows: King Agathocles of Sicily, a poor potter's son; Iphicrates, an Athenian general, son of a cobbler; Emperor

Aelius Pertinax, and Marcus Aurelius, sons of weavers; and Emperor Diocletian, son of a bookbinder.[3]

The novel presents some of the trials of the artisan as well as his success and festivities. The clothworkers present to the king a petition stating the difficulty of selling cloth, and requesting permission to traffic with foreign countries. Cardinal Wolsey, at that time Lord Chancellor, and a bitter foe to artisans, delays the granting of the petition. This is partly because of his hearing of a statement from Jack to the effect that the cardinal would never have his present position had his father (a butcher) been as slow in killing a calf as Wolsey is in granting poor men's suits. This reflection on the cardinal's low birth causes Wolsey to imprison the clothiers for a time. Their petition, however, is finally granted.

Not only the chief figures in Deloney's novels, but also some of the incidental persons are represented as rising from humble positions to eminence, partly through their own merits and partly through good fortune. An instance is in the story of Pert, a former draper, who is imprisoned because of his debts to several persons, including Jack. Jack, now a burgess for Newbury, sees Pert at work as a porter, and gives him capital to furnish a draper's shop again. He prospers, becoming sheriff and finally alderman.

Many disconnected stories abound, some of them dealing with horseplay and introducing popular well known individuals, such as Will Sommers, the court

---

[3] Similarly, in Heywood's *If You Know not Me, You Know Nobody*, Gresham and his friends are shown pictures of illustrious citizens who were formerly poor craftsmen. In this sentimental passage, tears of admiration are brought to their eyes, and ambition to be remembered after death is aroused.

fool. The unity of such a work as *Jack of Newbury* is to be found not in plot, but in the constant dealing with weavers and clothiers, and in the personality and influence of Jack.

In *Thomas of Reading,* also, we have a collection of many loosely connected stories, centering approximately about the following clothiers: Thomas Cole of Reading, Tom Dove of Exeter, Gray of Gloucester, William Fitzallen of Worcester, Sutton of Salisbury, Simon of Southampton, Hodgkins of Halifax, Cutbert of Kendall, and Martin Briam of Manchester. As the previously described novel, this one is full of antiquarian interest. It has apparently a greater proportion of fiction, although Cole is mentioned by historians; e. g., in Fuller's *Worthies of England;* Coates' *History of Reading* mentions him as a rich clothier. The novel treats certain clothing centers and popular clothiers that have become associated with these.

Certain interesting parallels to *Jack of Newbury* may be mentioned. There are several instances in which the clothiers entertain one of the royal family; e. g., on one occasion[4] the two princes, William and Robert, and on another[5] King Henry I, at Worcester, who "returned to London, with great joy of his Commons."

A somewhat more important parallel is one in which the clothiers make various requests to the king. One of these is that all cloth measures be standardized, a matter which is settled by the king's calling the length of his own arm a yard and the standard.[6] Another

---

[4] Chapter 5.   [5] Chapter 7.
[6] Another tradition states that a yard was the length of another king's arm, that of Edward I.

request is that people may be made to take as current
the cracked coins of which the clothiers have a store.
A third request is that those who rob clothiers may
instantly be hanged. All these requests are granted.

Still another comparison with *Jack of Newbury* is
in the picture of the substantial and prosperous Thomas
Cole of Reading. We do not get the presentation of
the clothiers at work, as we did in the case of the
weavers. But Cole is said to have daily in his house
a hundred men servants and forty maids; he maintains
two or three hundred people, spinners and carders, and
many householders.

The clothiers were an honored livery company.
Though the trade was last of the twelve great ones,
this novel attempts to show that it was an eminent
and respectable calling; it was the chief craft, dealing
with the greatest merchandise; the younger sons of
knights and gentlemen who inherited no land, generally took to this trade.[7] A story in the novel that
illustrates this is that of the Earl of Shrewsbury's
daughter, Margaret, who, left resourceless, is adopted
by Gray's wife as an apprentice. She is untrained for
any manual work, but reveals her high breeding in the
fact that she can read and write; she is, therefore,
apprenticed to an honorable craft.

Thomas of Reading is interesting and important because of its influence on several other works. Three
non-extant plays dealing with clothiers are supposed,
in the main, to be based on this novel as a source.

Deloney's *Gentle Craft*, Part 1, 1597; and Part 2,
perhaps early in 1598, deals with shoemakers, the
popular guild of the late 16th century. The prevailing

[7] This is brought out in Deloney's introduction.

attitude in literature toward this guild is kindlier than toward most crafts, even the great livery companies. The novel is rich in the agreeable features also seen in the other two novels, such as a spirit of fraternity, cheerfulness, folk stories and realistic treatment of the artisans' lives. Important figures are Crispine and Crispianus, celebrated in chapbooks, ballads, plays, and pageants. The story used is drawn from the familiar patron saint legend.

Substantial shoemakers are Richard Casteler, who, because of his industry and early rising, is called "Cock of Westminster," and who contributes to the poor of Westminster and forty pounds to the poor children of Christ's Hospital;[8] Peachy, a Fleet Street shoemaker, who has forty tall workmen besides apprentices, whom he has wait on him on holidays with sword and buckler;[9] and Simon Eyre.

The story of Simon Eyre and his rise from poverty as a London shoemaker's apprentice to riches and the position of Mayor of London, is one which may distort actual truth as the story of Whittington does, in claiming that the latter was of low birth.

"Albeit he descended from mean parentage, yet, by God's blessing, in the end he came to be a most worthy man in the commonwealth."

A story of Eyre's early life is associated with a folk story of interest. On Sunday morning it was the apprentices' custom to breakfast on pudding-pies (i. e., puddings of baked meats). One Sunday, Eyre, having no money "to pay the shot" (i. e., his share of the ex-

___

[8] Thomas Deloney's *The Gentle Craft*. Part 2. Edited by A. F. Lange.
[9] Part 2.

pense), borrows from the others, promising that if ever he becomes Lord Mayor of London, he will give a breakfast to all London apprentices. This is, of course, realized in the Shrove Tuesday pancake feast. Another feature of the story is interesting and typical of a number of self-made craftsmen, as Whittington, and Thornton in Brewer's *The Love-Sick King;* i. e., they have a premonition in their days of youth and poverty that they will some day become famous.

Having served his apprenticeship, Eyre gets a shop and marries. His marriage is very fortunate, for his wife is a good assistant to him in his work. Her interest is especially in his welfare, as we shall see later.

He hires a French journeyman, who tries to persuade him to buy a certain cargo of five thousand pounds worth of lawns, cambric, and other articles of linen, commodities very rare in London at that time. His wife also persuades him to bargain with the Greek merchant for the cargo, and to say that he does so in behalf of one of the chief aldermen in the city.

"For in the morning thou shalt go to him in thy doublet of sheep's skins, with a smuched face, and thy apron before thee, thy thumb leather and hand-leather buckled close to thy wrist, with a foule band about thy neck, and a greasie cap on thy head."[10]

She tells him that he must afterwards dress like an alderman to give an impression of dignity and wealth, having a beard fashioned like an alderman's, a fair doublet of tawny satin with a damask cassock that is furred about the skirts, breeches of black velvet, a white band about the neck, cuffs on the wrists, a black velvet gown, and gloves on his hands, and a gold ring

[10] Page 67.

on his forefinger. This pictures well the dress of an
alderman, an official that ambitious craftsmen strove
to become, and illustrates, together with the above
quoted passage, Deloney's interest in clothing and his
skill in describing it. His wife, moreover, will have
the handsome barber accompany him to the merchant,
as if he were his man. The deceptive plan is successful; Eyre succeeds in purchasing the cargo on credit,
all steps having been laid out by his wife.

The Mayor and the Mayoress invite the Eyres to
supper. Eyre's wife is especially proud of associating
with the mayor and other great ones, and talks about
it to her friends, her pride consisting chiefly in the fact
that her husband is "the rich shoemaker that bought
all the goods in the great argozy:"

" 'Of a truth,' quoth she, 'although I sate closely by my ladie's
side, I could eat nothing for very joy to heare and see that we
were so much made of. And never give me credit, husband, if
I did not hear the officers whisper as they stood behind me and
all demanded one of another what you were and what I was.
"O," quoth one, "do you see this man. Mark him well, and
marke his wife well, that simple woman that sits next my ladie
— what are they?" "What are they?" quoth another. "Marry,
this is the rich shoomaker that bought all the goods in the great
argozy. I tell you there was never such a shoomaker seen in
London since the city was builded." "Now, by my faith," quoth
the third, "I have heard much of him to-day among the merchants in the street, going between the Two Chains." Credit
me, husband, of mine honesty this was their communications.
Nay, and do you not remember, when the rich citizen drank to
you — which craved pardon because he knew not your name —
what my Lord Maior said? "Sir," quoth he, "his name is Master
Eyer." Did you mark that? And presently thereupon he added
these words: "this is the gentleman that bought" — and so forth.
"The gentleman" — understood you? Did you heare him speake
that word?'

" 'In troth, wife.' quoth he, 'my lord uttered many good words of me, I thank his Honour, but I heard not that.'

" 'No?' quoth she. 'I heard it well enough, for by and by he proceeded further, saying: "I suppose, though he sit here in simple sort, he is more sufficient to beare this charge than myselfe." Yea, thought I, he may thank his wife for that, if it come so to passe.' "[11]

This excellent passage compares with some of the best delineations in drama. Condensed as it is, abounding in key words, as "gentleman," "lady," "merchant," and expressions, as "I have heard much of him today among the merchants," and "he is more sufficient to beare this charge than myselfe;" i. e., the mayoralty, it portrays an aspiring craftswoman, a type which is treated much in drama of the early 17th century. But there is this feature about her that differentiates her from some of the craftsmen's wives portrayed by Jonson, Marston, and Massinger, and Dekker's Dame Margery in *The Shoemakers' Holiday*. Her interest is less in gay clothing and ceremonies than in the fact that she and her husband have actually accomplished something of note. Keen and energetic as she is, she hears such words as those quoted above, and thinking not of empty titles and fancy raiment alone, she regards such talk as a harbinger of future success, a view which is entirely overlooked by her dull and passive husband. Dekker shifts the emphasis in his Dame Margery to an interest in gorgeous attire, not in commercial enterprise. The initiative in Dekker's play is in Eyre.

Eyre speculates in various commodities and becomes very rich. Offered the position of sheriff, he is re-

[11] Pages 71 and 72.

luctant to take so great a place. His wife, however, is always at hand to encourage him. She calls to his attention his great wealth, and appeals to his religion and patriotism: "You have enough to discharge the place whereunto you are called, with credit, and wherefore sendeth God goods but therewithall to do him and your country service?"[12]

Eyre is chosen mayor and becomes a draper. In accordance with his youthful vow, he invites, on Shrove Tuesday, the apprentices to a pancake breakfast in his own house. He builds Leadenhall, where there is a market every Monday for leather, where shoemakers may buy of tanners.

Deloney's *Gentle Craft*, as was stated before, is in part the source of several plays; e. g., Dekker's *Shoemakers' Holiday*, 1599. In this play, Eyre is represented as very industrious, bustling, and humorous, far more realistic than the puppet figure of Deloney. The fact of his having so many journeymen is an indication of success, since these were expensive; many masters could afford only apprentices. Eyre buys from a ship captain a certain commodity[13] which eventually enriches him. He is made sheriff, and later (partly because of the death of certain aldermen) Lord Mayor of London. Unlike Gresham or Thornton, Eyre is indifferent as to forms, ceremony, or display. Indeed, the early part of the play does not present him as ever expecting to be Mayor. Entertaining the King at a banquet, he is not in the least abashed nor excited (as many tradespeople would be) in the presence

---

[12] Page 79.
[13] The purchase of the commodity is slurred over in Dekker's play; in Deloney's novel, on the other hand, it is given some elaboration.

of royalty. The king calls the building, erected in Cornhill by Eyre, "Leaden Hall," because Eyre found, in digging for it, the lead to cover it. He also grants to the shoemakers, at the request of Eyre, a patent to hold two market days for leather in Leaden Hall.

Eyre is one of the most natural and carefree of men, one who is well described by a nobleman to the king:

> Your grace will think when you behold the man,
> Hee's rather a wild Ruffian than a Maior;
> Yet thus much Ile ensure your Majestie,
> In all his actions that concerns his state,
> He is as serious, provident, and wise
> As full of gravitie amongst the grave,
> As any Maior hath been these many yeares.[14]

Eyre's vow to give the apprentices a pancake breakfast on Shrove-Tuesday reappears here. He fulfils this vow out of a spirit of fraternity for his workmen, not out of any special love for display. The apprentices call Shrove-Tuesday Saint Hugh's Holiday.[15]

The interesting theme of speculation may be briefly touched on. It draws us away somewhat from a study of handicraftsmen, but is still connected with their aspirations and ideals, for the artisans in this literature are desirous of becoming famous speculators. The opening lines of Marlowe's *Jew of Malta*, Salarino's poetic speech in *The Merchant of Venice*,[16] and parts of Fletcher and Massinger's *Beggars' Bush*, 1622, portray with imaginative force the power of the successful merchant, and also the dangers that he has to undergo.

[14] Volume 1 of 1873 edition of Dekker, p. 70.
[15] Dekker's *Shoemakers' Holiday* will be described more fully later.
[16] Act 1, sc. 3.

Speculation is often closely associated with the founding of institutions, such as colleges or hospitals. This is usually accomplished only by the mature and successful speculator, but even the ambitious apprentice or craftsman's son frequently looks forward to embodying his dreams in the founding of some building. Cromwell in *Thomas Lord Cromwell*, 1602, the young son of a Putney blacksmith, is conscious of future greatness:

> I'll build a palace where this cottage stands,
> As fine as is King Henry's house at Sheen.[17]

William Rowley's *New Wonder, or A Woman Never Vexed*, pr. 1632, deals with the foundation in 1197 by Walter Brune, a merchant, of the Hospital of Our Lady; and with the enlarging and bettering of Ludgate Prison in the 15th century by Stephen Foster, the mayor (son of a fishmonger), and Agnes, his wife. Abounding in absurdities and anachronisms, the play is interesting as illustrative of the pomp that attended any civic institution.

Two plays that deal with Thomas Gresham, grocer, the founder of the Royal Exchange, are *Byrsa Basilica*,[18] a Latin play written by J. Rickets in 1570; and Thomas Heywood's *If You Know Not Me, You Know Nobody*, Part 2, 1606. The latter portrays Gresham as a typical self-made man between whom and the nobly born man there is an enmity. Vicissitudes of the speculator are well represented here.

One day Gresham and his friends are caught in a storm. The inconvenience caused him calls to his mind

---

[17] Act 1, sc. 2.
[18] A description of the play is in *Jahrbuch der Deutschen Shakespeare Gesellschaft*, vol. 34, p. 281.

the desirability of having a roofed exchange for merchants to transact business in; he resolves that he shall establish such a one. In a sentimental manner, Heywood describes how Gresham and his friends are shown pictures of charitable citizens, merchants and craftsmen, such as Sir John Allen, Sir Richard Whittington, mercers who benefited their country in various ways. Gresham and his friends are moved to tears of admiration, and Gresham fervently declares that he will build an Exchange, so that he will be remembered after death. The building is finally erected with much ceremony and pomp. Gresham, the Mayor, and sheriffs lay gold on top of the first bricks. The queen herself and the ambassadors are entertained by Gresham.[19] She calls the place the Royal Exchange and knights Gresham.

Gresham is throughout the play a strange combination of altruism and worldliness; he is utilitarian, is interested in useful trades and pursuits, but his industry has as its goal the placing of him in the public view. On thinking of the future craftsmen who will transact business in the Exchange, he says:

> Some shall prove masters, and speak in Gresham's praise,
> In Gresham's work we did our fortunes raise.[20]

Certain plays that deal with craftsmen becoming local Mayors are *The Mayor of Quinborough*, of uncertain date and authorship (perhaps largely by Middleton), which tells how the witty tanner, Simon, becomes Mayor of Quinborough; and Anthony Brewer's

[19] Heywood follows Stow's description. *Annals*, p. 1131, the companies in their liveries await the Queen's progress.

[20] Shakespeare Soc. Pub., vol. 6, p. 107, l. 10-12.

Love-Sick King, 1605.[21] The latter play, like many in
its class, has a number of improbabilities and anachronisms. It pictures a poor Newcastle peddler, whose
sole possessions are needles and a lambs-skin, selling
his lambs-skin for a groat, investing the latter in a
commodity of iron ore which later turns out to be an
ore of gold. With his wealth, Thornton builds a wall,
a hundred feet high and twelve in breadth, around
Newcastle, and reëdifies Allhallows Church.

This play should be considered together with a lost
play, *The History of Richard Whittington*, 1605, dealing with a historical character and one far more celebrated as a popular hero than Thornton.

According to popular stories[22] and a charming ballad,
Sir Richard Whittington's Advancement, the main
facts of Whittington's life are as follows: He is a
poor boy[23] of Lancashire who is taken by a London
mercer to serve him as a scullion. Disgusted with his
low estate he runs away, but the London bells give
him heart again:

> London's bells sweetly rung
> Whittington's back return;
> Evermore sounding so,
> Turn again, Whittington;
> For thou, in time, shall grow
> Lord Mayor of London.[24]

So he returns to his apprenticeship. The master is
about to sail away to speculate with his merchandise.
Whittington "ventures" his sole possession, a cat, on

---

[21] Edited by A. E. H. Swaen.
[22] Variants of the story will not be considered here.
[23] He was of well-to-do parents, bound apprentice to a mercer,
the mercers being the foremost of the twelve great companies.
[24] From the ballad, *The History of Sir Richard Whittington's
Advancement*. It is in Percy Socy. Pubs., vol. 1.

this voyage. The cat is taken to a country which is badly troubled with rats and mice. The king, therefore, gives "heaps of gold" for the cat. Whittington becomes a speculating merchant, marries his master's daughter, becomes sheriff, and three times Lord Mayor of London. He lends generously of his wealth to the king to carry on war in France, and is kind to poor people and widows. He founds Whittington College, and gives to Newgate Prison.

The non-extant play, in all probability, took a similar form to the story just described, since dramatists tend to follow popular tradition rather than history. Assuming, then, that this was the general trend of the lost play, one may see several parallels between *The Love-Sick King* and *The History of Richard Whittington.* Each came poor, as was popularly but erroneously supposed, a stranger to a large town. There is in each an anticipation of future wealth and greatness. Thornton's whisperings in the ear correspond to the agreeably prophetic bells of the Whittington story. Each begins his speculation with a trifling article: Thornton with a lambs-skin, Whittington with a cat, objects which are afterward associated with their names. Thornton is ridiculed because of his humble lambs-skin, as Whittington very probably is because of his cat. Each becomes unexpectedly rich and eminent because of his peculiar venture. Each marries a relative of his former master. Each becomes Mayor in the town of his prosperity, one in Newcastle, the other in London. Each remembers the poor, and contributes something to the nation and to individual poor people. Brewer apparently attempts, on the suggestion of the Whittington play, to arouse for Thornton an admiration equal to that long since held for Whittington.[25]

On first considering these two treatments of enterprising craftsmen and traders, one might consider that both should be relegated to the nursery with *Cinderella, Puss in Boots,* and similar specimens of fairy lore. But, however improbable they are, they may have a basis in possibility, as reflecting some typical Elizabethan merchant under the guise of a medieval one. The Elizabethan period is one which shows many vicissitudes in trade as well as in other kinds of fortune. A rich merchant might suddenly lose all he had; on the other hand, one with almost nothing might become successful. The original article ventured might be a cat, a lambs-skin, or almost anything. The story of Whittington's cat is not wholly impossible, as cats were greatly in demand in some parts of the world. A possible explanation of the rumors in regard to the cat and the lambs-skin is that these commodities reaped a fair amount of profit for the speculators; with that profit they made more, and gradually became rich. For the purpose of drama and ballad, however, it is more convenient to state that "heaps of gold" were given for a cat.

The names of craftsmen were perpetuated not only in the buildings that they contributed toward erecting, but also in certain verse epitaphs. One of the best of these is *An Epitaph of Maister Frances Benison.*[26] His success as a haberdasher and philanthropist is commented on.

[25] A number of these features of comparison have been mentioned by Swaen in his edition of Brewer's play.

[26] It is in Collmann's *Ballads and Broadsides,* p. 79. Many other similar epitaphs are in this volume.

A combination of the craftsman's interest in spectacular exhibitions and of his pride in civic distinctions
is to be found in the Lord Mayor's Show.[27] Devised,
for the most part, by poets and dramatists in sympathy with craftsmen, these spectacles present the
mayors rather as what they aspire to than as what
they frequently are; as merchant-adventurers rather
than as handicraftsmen. There is, then, much opportunity for imaginative and poetic representation, a
representation, which, because of the clumsy and in-
congruous physical devices of these pageants, arouses
much satire and burlesque on the part of later poets
and dramatists.

The Lord Mayor's Show, celebrating the Mayor's
investiture in office, at its height in the reign of
James I, is an outgrowth in the middle of the 16th
century of the Midsummer Show.[28] The following
procedure, as outlined by Nathan Drake, is typical of
all Lord Mayor Shows.

On the day of St. Simon and St. Jude, October 28th,
the Mayor, having been chosen from one of the twelve
great livery companies, enters office. On the next day,
October 29th, he goes by barge decorated with the
city's arms, toward Westminster. Near him goes the
Queen's barge with the mayor's arms on it. "Next
before him" goes the barge of the livery of his own
company and of some trading company, as the merchant-adventurers. Each company goes in order with

[27] Collections of these shows are in F. W. Fairholt's *Lord
Mayors' Pageants*, vol. 10 of the Percy Society Publications.
Good criticisms of them are in R. Withington's *English Pageantry*, 2 volumes.
[28] The Midsummer Show was a pageantic ceremony, combin-
ing religious allegory with folk-lore and civic celebration.

its proper barge. The mercer's company is always first, with its huge representation of the Virgin; this order is always kept, except that the company of which the mayor of that year is free is always second. The twelve companies are often used to represent pillars of the commonwealth or the twelve seasons. At Westminster, the mayor takes the oath of office, and then returns by water to Paul's Wharf through Cheapside. They pass on horseback with pomp and music to Guildhall, where they dine. The new and old mayor ride on horseback, both in scarlet gowns, and the latter with a gold chain about his neck. Aldermen follow in two's, all in scarlet; those who were former mayors wear gold chains.[29]

Beginning with 1585, the dramatists, especially Munday, Middleton, Dekker, and Heywood, become the writers of the poetry for the spectacles. Trade symbolism is frequently stressed; e. g., in Peele's *Decensus Astraeae*, 1585, the mayor, who is a skinner, is dressed like a Moor and rides on a lynx. Certain trade properties, such as the Golden Fleece for the drapers, the goldsmith's forge for the goldsmiths, the Lemnian forge for the ironmongers, fur bearing animals for the skinners, and the Virgin for the mercers, become established. Certain stock personages proper to each company; i. e., formerly free of that company, and representing valor, industry, altruism, and nationalism, appear whenever that company has its mayoralty show. Of special interest in this connection are the heroic figures, Sir Francis Drake, *England's True Jason*,[30]

[29] *English Pageantry*, vol. II, p. 13.
[30] The drapers' Lord Mayor's Show affords opportunities for introducing much imaginative poetry; e. g., in Heywood's *Porta*

Sir John Hawkwood, and Sir William Walworth, free of the drapers', tailors', and fishmongers' company respectively.[31]

Inasmuch as the Lord Mayor's Show was stereotyped, for the most part, the subject may be best treated by considering with some care one of the best and most representative of the Lord Mayor's Shows; i. e., Dekker's *London's Tempe*, 1629.[32] In this work, which was written in 1629 for the Honorable James Campbell, mayor and ironmonger, there is much emphasis on the craft and its commercial significance. Dekker unites the charm and fascination in constructive labor with the more popular poetic presentation of a craft's worldwide significance and importance. The glory and romance of the merchant-adventurers are also introduced.

Dekker begins by giving some history of the Lord Mayor's Show. There follows a water show, presenting Oceanus, crowned, in a silver scallop shell drawn by two sea-horses. He glorifies the Thames and London:

> New Troy's towers on tiptoe rize
> To hit heaven's roofe.

The second show presents a sea on which is a sea-lion, because it is one of the supporters of the East India Company, of which the Mayor is free. Tethys rides on the lion. The third show presents an estridge biting a horseshoe.

Pietatis, 1638, there is the following praise of the sheep:

> Of patience, and of profit th' emblem is,
> In former ages by the heroes sought;
> After from Greece into Hesperia brought;
> She's cloth'd in plenteous riches, and being shorne,
> Her fleece an order and by emperours worne.

[31] Hawkwood and Walworth have been already discussed in Johnson's *Nine Worthies of London*.

[32] Percy Socy. Pubs., vol. 10, *The Lord Mayor's Pageant*.

The fourth show is the most interesting to us, because of its bearing on the ironmongers' trade and work. It presents the Lemnian forge at which are Vulcan, the smith, and his servans, the Cyclopes, working on the anvils. The smiths sing to the sounding of the anvil in praise of iron:

> Brave iron, brave hammer, from your sound,
> The art of musicke has her ground;
> On the anvile thou keep'st time,
> Thy knick-a-knock is a smithes best chyme.
>
> Yet thwick-a-thwack,
> Thwick, thwacka-thwack, thwack,
> Make our brawny sinews crack,
> Then pit-a-pat pat, pit-a-pat,
> Till thickest barres be beaten flat.
>
> We shooe the horses of the sunne,
> Harness the dragons of the moone,
> Forge Cupid's quiver, bow and arrowes,
> And our dame's coach that's drawn with sparrowes.
> Till thwick-a-thwack, etc.[33]

The passage has onomatopoetic value, suggesting by its sound the hammering on the anvil. The manifold uses of iron are also mentioned: it is used in the manufacture of implements of war, ships, bulwarks, furnaces, and tools for practically all trades. The dialogue between Jove and Vulcan, though undramatic, is interesting on account of its praise of iron:

[33] Cf. Whittier's *Shoemakers.*

> "Rap, rap! upon the well worn stone
> How falls the polished hammer!
> Rap, rap! the measured sound has grown
> A quick and merry clamor."

In Jordan's *The Cheaters Cheated,* are lines on ironmongers.

Iron, best of metals, pride of minerals.
Hart of the earth, hand of the world, which fals
Heavy when it strikes home. By iron's strong charmes
Ryots lye bound. Warre stops her rough allarmes.
Iron, earthquakes strikes in foes; knits friends in love;
Iron's that mainehinge on which the world doth move;
No kingdomes globe can turne, even, smooth and round,
But that his axletree in iron is found;
For armies wanting iron are puffes of wind,
And but for iron, who, thrones of peace would mind?[34]

The imitative and the childish tendencies of artisans
have frequently been mentioned. The spectacle of the
Lord Mayor's Show, therefore, played a large part in
the imagination of artisans and citizens, and may have
had an influence on their love of acting and mimicry.
The mayor, with gold chain[35] and scarlet robe, on horseback, the procession, the spectacles, and the homage
paid to former greatness lingered in the imagination
of the bourgeois class, especially the craftsmen's wives
and apprentices. Each apprentice with ambition cher-
ished the dim possibility that he would become, in the
indefinite future, Lord Mayor. The homage paid, however, was chiefly to the outward ceremonies (the aver-
age craftsman regarding the Mayor and aldermen as
a boy does a procession of soldiers) and was inclined

[34] Cf. Whittier's *Shipbuilders.*
"Up,- Up,- in nobler toil than ours
No craftsmen bear a part;
We make of nature's giant powers
The slaves of human art."
[35] Interest in material representations of grandeur and greatness are also manifested in Murley, the brewer, in Drayton and
Munday's *Sir John Oldcastle.* He is prevailed on, through the
promise of knighthood, to give freely of his wealth. The golden
spurs which represented knighthood are fondled by him as toys
would be by a child.

to disregard the trying and responsible nature of the office.

Such a highly spectacular and bombastic ceremony was naturally subject to ridicule and burlesque. Beaumont and Fletcher's *Knight of the Burning Pestle* ridicules the love of craftsmen for pomp and glory. The Lord Mayor's Show and its clumsy wooden representations are ridiculed in Shirley's *A Contention for Honor and Riches,* 1633, and *Honoria and Mammon,* 1652. Several ballads; e. g., *Oh, London is a fine Town,* describe the clumsy imitations of nobility on the part of craftsmen.

As a conclusion, the Lord Mayor's Show may be said to be a very old ceremony, and one that still exists in certain sections of the world. Although it is true that each company vaunted itself over all others in its Lord Mayor's Show, nevertheless, co-operation and mutual support on the part of all the companies, especially of the twelve great ones, were stressed. Extravagant and spectacular to the extreme, the Lord Mayor's Show had, nevertheless, a place in art; and, in its insistence on justice, fraternity, co-operation, industry, and patriotism, it upheld the original idea and purpose of the guild system.

CHAPTER III

THE CRAFTSMAN AND HIS WORK

Before considering craftsmen at work it will be interesting to discuss a few charming ballads in which they appear. Two fantastic ballads are *The Merry Pranks of Robin Goodfellow*,[1] Robin Goodfellow being a fairy apprentice to a tailor; and *The Miller and the King's Daughter*.[2] We shall discuss Elizabethan ballads far more realistic than these which still border on folklore, though to a lesser extent than medieval ballads do. They present sovereigns traveling incognito, like Haroun Alraschid, among citizens. These ballads have a fresh, out-of-door atmosphere. They deal with the advancement of craftsmen, and their favorite theme; i. e., that of being associated with royalty. The advancement of these craftsmen is not dependent on any artistic skill or initiative on their part, but on sheer good fortune; hence these ballads differ from that on Whittington.

King James I and the Tinker[3] was apparently written during the reign of James I. The mender of kettles and lover of ale meets the king whom he does not know; they drink healths to each other. The tinker expresses his desire to see the king, who is hunting on the border. He is greatly surprised to find that this

[1] Percy Socy. Pub., vol. 2.
[2] Jamieson's *Popular Ballads and Songs*, vol. 1, p. 315.
[3] Percy Socy. Pub., vol. 17, p. 109.

stranger is the king. The sovereign is so pleased with
the tinker that he gives him money and land, and
knights him. The tinker's pride in his craft is expressed in the last stanza:

> Sir John of the Dale he has land, he has fee,
> At the court of the king who so happy as he?
> Yet still in his Hall hangs the tinker's old sack,
> And the budget of tools which he bore at his back.

Several charming ballads deal with millers and
present them as substantial and prosperous citizens.
An instance is *The Miller in his best array*.[4] It presents
a prosperous miller who rides singing to Manchester
to woo a baker's daughter. The other suitors from the
artisan ranks, however, are delineated somewhat better
than the miller. Thus, the glover borders his gloves
with bleeding hearts pierced with darts. The butcher
woos her, but she is afraid that he may dress her as
he does a calf. The tailor woos her, promising her rich
clothing and strange fashions. The miller wins her by
talking of his wealth and mill, but especially by teach-
ing her "to daunce a downe."

Two companion ballads make interesting illustrations
of this type, and present variety in characterization.
These are: *A pleasant new Ballad of the Miller of
Mansfield in Sherwood and of King Henry the Seconde*[5]
and *A Merry Ballad of the Miller and King Henry the
second*.[6] Neither of these Elizabethan ballads has relation to actual history; it is hardly conceivable that an
aristocratic Norman king could fraternize, as the one
in the ballad does, with a miller. The first ballad

---

[4] Shirburn Ballads, p. 116.   [5] Shirburn Ballads, p. 216.
[6] Shirburn Ballads, p. 311.

tells how the king, after hunting in Sherwood Forest, is feasted by a miller and his wife, though unknown to them. The second describes how the king rewards the miller's hospitality by inviting him and his family to court.

There is still another craftsman about whom and his associations with a king several stories and ballads were concerned; i. e., the tanner of Tamworth. His story somewhat resembles those just narrated of the tinker and the miller and their friendship with kings.[7] In one respect, however, the Elizabethan ballad to be described is of far more importance for our study; it skillfully delineates the tanner as such. It is, therefore, the first of these ballads just considered to fuse romanticism with realism.

A merye, pleasant and delectable history between Kinge Edward IV, and a Tanner of Tamworth, 1600,[8] depicts in Part 1 a well dressed and prosperous tanner, a member of one of the richer crafts. He is on horseback, wearing a good russet coat and sitting on a cowhide. He meets the King in hunting attire who asks the way to Drayton Basset. The surly tanner will

---

[7] Besides these ballads, Heywood's *King Edward IV* treats the figure.

[8] Arber's *Stationers' Register*, vol. 3, p. 173; Roxburghe Ballads, vol. 2, p. 163. It is in two parts.

The King and the Barker (Ritson's *Pieces of ancient popular poetry*, p. 61) is a medieval ballad describing a gruff tanner or barker who meets the king and thinks that the latter is a highwayman. However, they exchange horses, and the tanner is thrown from the horse. A final reconciliation results.

King Henry IV and the Tanner of Tamworth, 1564 (Stationers' Register, vol. 2, p. 338) and *King Edward IV and the Tanner of Tamworth,* 1586 (Stationers' Register, vol. 2, p. 45), are apparently on the same theme.

The Tanner of Tamworth also appears in Heywood's play, *King Edward IV.*

not direct him, and rudely refuses the king's invitation to a dinner, stating that he has more groats with him than the stranger has. Moreover, he takes the king for a thief who has stolen the lordly attire that he wears, and is perhaps trying to steal the tanner's valuable cowhide.

The second part describes how the king exchanges his steed for the tanner's mare, the tanner not forgetting, however (since he is suspicious of the king), to transfer his valuable cowhide to the steed that he is about to mount. After the tanner has seated himself on the back of the king's steed, the latter is so frightened by the black horns and black tail of the cowhide which he carries that he runs away with the tanner. The latter is heavily thrown, but soon recovers, to be dismayed at the five hundred lords and knights that have obeyed the summons of the king's bugle. Again he shows the zealous craftsman's interest in his work by fearing that they are all thieves who have come to steal his cowhide.

The king, revealing himself to the tanner, is so pleased with the amusement that the latter has caused him that he gives him Plumpton Parke, three tenements, and five hundred pounds a year "to maintaine thy good cowhide." The tanner thanks him, saying:

> If ever thou comest to merry Tamworth,
> thou shalt have clouting leather for thy shone.

We have in this ballad, then, a good portrait of a substantial tanner, proud of his trade, whose precious cowhide is the direct cause of the humorous accident which he suffers.

In considering realistic descriptions of manual

workers in poetry, one cannot afford to overlook a vivid presentation by Spenser of smelters. Spenser, it is true, was little concerned with craftsmen, nor are smelters to be strictly considered artists or craftsmen; but the varied appeal of the following description of the workers in Mammon's cave to sight and feeling is hardly excelled by any other description of labor:

> And every feend his busie paines applyde
> To melt the golden metall, ready to be tryde.
>
> One with great bellows gathered filling ayre,
> And with forst wind the fewell did inflame;
> Another did the dying bronds repayre
> With yron tongs, and sprinckled ofte the same
> With liquid waves, fiers Vulcans rage to tame,
> Who, maystring them, renewd his former heat:
> Some scumd the drosse that from the metall came;
> Some stird the molten owre with ladles great:
> And every one did swincke, and every one did sweat.[9]

The verse description of Jack of Newbury's workshop anticipates the modern factory system. In a large room two hundred men are each working at a loom. A boy is beside each man, making quills on which the weavers wind the thread which forms the woof of cloth. A hundred singing women card or comb the wool. In another room two hundred girls are spinning and singing. A hundred and fifty poor children separate the coarse from the fine wool. Fifty shearmen clip the nap from the cloth. There are eighty rowers, whose task is to roughen the cloth. Forty men work in a dye-house and twenty in a fulling mill.[10]

[9] Spenser's *Faerie Queene*, Book 2, Canto 7, part of stanza 35 and stanza 36.

[10] Cleansing and thickening are done in the fulling mill.

The weavers' song represents the cheerful atmosphere of the shop. The singers look back to a golden age in which great heroes like Hercules were spinners, in which princes were shepherds and queens were bakers, and in which concord abounded but envy did not exist. Following is a stanza of the song.

When Hercules did use to spin,
And Pallas wrought upon the loome,
Then Love and Friendship did agree
To keep the bands of amity.

King Henry VIII who is visiting Jack's establishment, is presented by the workmen with a gilt beehive and golden bees[11] to represent a commonwealth and its industrious artisans. The king is greatly pleased with Jack's industrial system.

In *Thomas of Reading* the clothiers are not described at work, but Cole's substantiality is evident. He has a hundred men servants and forty maids, several hundred spinners and carders.

An interesting inventory of the shoemakers' tools, given in Deloney's *Gentle Craft*, Part 1, deserves a few words of introduction, as it is associated with a tradition dear to the shoemakers' guild. Hugh, a Welsh prince and shoemaker's apprentice, becomes a religious martyr. His fellow shoemakers visit and comfort him in prison; he expresses his gratitude toward their chivalry and kindliness by singing a song in their honor, and calling them the Gentle Craft. The shoemakers regard him as a saint, and after his martyrdom make their tools out of his bones, this being the

[11] The simile of the commonwealth and the bees is also in Hobbes' *Leviathan* and Shakespeare's *Henry V*, not to mention other parallels, outside of our period.

hypothetical origin of the expression, "St. Hugh's bones," as applied to the tools on the back of a journey-man shoemaker. The words of the shoemakers are as follows:

And mark what St. Hughe's bones shall be:
First a drawer and a dresser;
Two wedges, a more and a lesser;
A pretty block three inches high,
In fashion squared like a die,
Which shall be called by proper name
A heel-block; the very same,
A hand-leather, and a thumb-leather likewise,
To pull our shoo-thread, we must devise;
The needle and the thimble shall not be left alone,
The pincers and the pricking-aule, and the rubbing-stone;
The aule-steele and tackes, the sow-haires beside,
The stirrop, holding fast while we sowe the cowhide;
The whetstone, the stopping-stick, and the paring-knife—
All this doth belong to a journeyman's life.
Our apron is the shrine to wrap these bones in:
Thus shrowd we Saint Hugh in gentle lamb's skin.[12]

Several ballads enter, to some extent, into a humor-ous description of the making of beer. Instances are *Allan O'Maut*,[13] *John Barleycorn*,[14] and *A Pleasant New Ballad of the Bloody Murther of Sir John Barley-Corn*.[15]

The last of these will serve as an illustration. Barleycorn is ploughed, but revives after rain. He is then cut down and bound like a thief. After being stacked and beaten until the flesh falls from his bones, he is fanned and sifted, steeped in a vat, dried over

---

[12] Deloney's *The Gentle Craft*, Part 1, chap. 4.
[13] Jamieson's *Popular Ballads and Songs*, vol. 2, p. 237.
[14] Jamieson's *Popular Ballads and Songs*, vol. 2, p. 240.
[15] Jamieson's *Popular Ballads and Songs*, vol. 2, p. 251.

a fire, ground in a mill, and boiled in a vat. He is finally stored in a barrel, and his blood drawn out through a tap.

In a few dramatic works, artisans are well delineated as workers. Unfortunately, though the drama is rich in photographic sketches of dishonest and disagreeable tradesfolk in their shops (in the plays especially of Middleton and the later ones of Dekker), we have very few plays besides Dekker's *Shoemakers' Holiday* and Rowley's *A Shoemaker a Gentleman* that skillfully interweave romance of pure and youthful love with the joy in craftsmanship.

These two important plays will now be considered, together with others that combine, to some extent, the romantic plot with the craft element. Dekker's *The Shoemakers' Holiday*, 1599, has already been considered from one viewpoint; i. e., that of the self-made man. A brief summary of the play will be given.

One plot is concerned with the love of Lacy, the thriftless Earl of Lincoln's son, for Rose, the daughter of the Lord Mayor of London. The two fathers are anxious to prevent such union of noble with base blood. Lacy is sent to fight against France, but remains in London disguised as a Dutch journeyman shoemaker, being finally hired by Simon Eyre.

The other plot deals with Eyre and his journeymen shoemakers. Ralph, one of these, is pressed for the war against France. He is not diffident himself about going to war, but Eyre and the other journeymen clamor at the thought that they shall lose so good a workman, and that Ralph's wife will be unsupported. Ralph, departing, gives his wife, Jane, a pair of shoes cut out by Hodge, stitched by Firke, seamed by himself, which he says he will always know from other shoes.[16]

The play abounds in humor and merriment. Dame Margery, Eyre's wife, constantly finds fault with the servants. Her imitation of fashionable people is vividly portrayed.[17] Lacy, singing in Dutch, is hired by Eyre, who is persuaded to do this by the journeymen. The latter wish to have such an amusing fellow to help the passing away of working hours. He furnishes amusement for them all, joins in their morris dance, in which he is discovered by Rose as he dances with other shoemakers. Later on, the father of Rose discovers her with Lacy. Rose, that the situation may be explained to her father, persuades Lacy to pretend that he is trying a pair of shoes on her, a ruse which succeeds.[18] The Mayor is greatly disgusted when he finds that his daughter has run off with a shoemaker.

The pathetic part, which somewhat resembles the *Enoch Arden* story, is concerned with Ralph and Jane. Jane is obliged to work in a sempster's shop, for, as Eyre had said to her on her husband's departure for war, "these prettie fingers must spin, must card, must worke." As she works, she is wooed by a citizen, Hammon, whom, though loving, she rejects, inasmuch as her husband may still be alive. His suit is well portrayed, although it may have too much sentiment. Moreover, the atmosphere of the shop is vividly pre-

[16] This is a beautiful dramatic touch; the shoes form a symbol of Ralph and Jane's union. It is to the credit of the play that the incident is made so vivid and introduced so early.

[17] She will be considered in the passage with aspiring craftswomen.

[18] It is strange that the idea occurs to her and not to him. Shoemaking was actually Lacy's trade once, when he was traveling in **Wittenberg**.

sented; the progress of his suit is worked in with the details of her work:

HAM. How prettily she workes, oh prettie hand!
      Oh happie worke.....
JANE. Sir, what ist you buy?
      What ist you lacke sir? callico, or lawne,
      Fine cambricke shirts, or bands, what will you buy?
HAM. That which thou wilt not sell, faith yet Ile trie:
      How do you sell this handkercher?
JANE. Good cheape.
HAM. And how these ruffles?
JANE. Cheape too.
HAM. All cheape, how sell you then this hand?
JANE. My hands are not to be sold.
HAM. To be given then, nay faith I come to buy.
JANE. But none knowes when.
      ....
HAM. Looke how you wound this cloth, so you wound me.[19]

By a false report that her Ralph was one of the soldiers killed in France, Jane is misled into consenting to marry Hammon.

Meanwhile, Ralph returns for war, lame, friendless, penniless, and homeless. The shoemakers, his comrades, welcome him back to his old work, but can give him no information as to the whereabouts of his wife. He receives, later, an order to make a pair of shoes on a certain model for a lady who is to be married shortly. The model consists of one of the shoes that Ralph had given his wife on leaving for war. He instantly recognizes the shoe:

[19] 1873 ed. of Dekker's *Dramatic Works*, vol. 1, p. 46. This courting somewhat reminds one of the poetic epistle of Drayton in which Shore, a goldsmith, shows King Edward IV all of his choice jewels for sale; but the fairest of all the jewels in the shop, his wife, Jane, is not for sale.

> this shoe I durst be sworne
> Once covered the instep of my Jane:
> This is her size, her breadth, thus trod my love,
> These true-love knots I prickt, I hold my life,
> But this old shooe I shall find out my wife.[20]

He gains the promise of the assistance of his fellow-journeymen. When he tries on the shoes for his wife, she does not recognize him; travel and lameness have changed him. But since he resembles Ralph, she gives him gold for Ralph's sake.

The journeymen shoemakers, armed with clubs, take Jane from Hammon and restore her to Ralph. Firk, the mischief-lover, to furnish further amusement, arranges it so that the Lord Mayor mistakes Ralph and Jane for the Dutch shoemaker and Rose, an error which protracts the comedy somewhat.

Something should be said about the excellent characterization of the craftsmen. Eyre and his three journeymen are all delineated as shoemakers, but each is differentiated from the others. Eyre is the bustling, energetic, humorous, but perfectly calm person, who, as he himself says, feels as young and hearty at fifty-six as he felt many years before. He has won and kept the good will of his workmen who are elated at his success and appointment as Mayor. Ralph is the serious, hard-working man, evidently a skilled artisan from what the others say about him. Hodge, who is made master of the shop after Eyre has become Mayor, has a vision of becoming Mayor, or Alderman, at least, in the future. Firk is the most interesting of the journeymen; he has a ready wit. True to its genre, the

[20] Page 54.

play presents his wit in form of terms most pertinent
to a craftsman:

> they shall be married together by
> this rush, or else turn Firk to a fir-
> kin of butter to tan leather withall.
> They shall be knit like a paire
> of stockings in matrimony.[21]

Firk is conscious of his own rank, that of second journeyman, and vies with Hodge in making shoes for great
ones, such as court ladies.[22] The base work; i. e., the
making of shoes for ordinary people, is given to Hans,
the new journeyman. Firk is somewhat vexed at the
fact that he, the elder journeyman, is called to breakfast after Hans, the new one.

The Shoemakers' Holiday is a composite of all the
most pleasing forms of literature on the crafts. There
is the old spirit of fraternity, illustrated in the journeymen's work in the shop, and in their united resolve
to help Ralph recover his wife. There is also the charming poetry of contentment in fellowship and mutual
labor; e. g., Second Three Men's Song, part of which
is as follows:

> Cold's the wind, and wet's the rain,
> Saint Hugh be our good speed,
> Ill is the weather that bringeth no gain,
> Nor helps good hearts in need.
>
> Trowl the bowl, the jolly nut-brown bowl,
> And here, kind mate, to thee;

[21] Pages 59, 60.
[22] Something that is emphasized in literature is the love that
craftsmen had of being associated with royalty or eminence,
either in the way of working for such high classes, or gaining
even a slight recognition from such, a nod from an earl or a king.

Let's sing a dirge for Saint Hugh's soul,
And down it merrily.[23]

Eyre's speech to Ralph, departing for war, touches on
the chivalric stories of craftsmen, and especially of
shoemakers in wars. There are technical details of the
craft, and frequent references to tools, such as stirrop,
heele-block, etc. The industrious and enterprising
craftsman is presented in the person of Simon Eyre.
Pathos is in the story of Ralph and Jane, and romantic
charm in this, in the Lacy-Rose story, and in the deer
hunt and morris dance. There is also a touch of satire
in Dame Margery's affectations, an anticipation of a
favorite later type of city wife. There are many highly
individualized tradesfolk. In short, the play portrays
charmingly the life, with its various joys and sorrows,
of the craftsman and craftswoman.

William Rowley's *A Shoemaker a Gentleman,*[24] 1609,
is almost as valuable a contribution to this genre as
is Dekker's play. Sources for the play are the first
two tales of the first part of Deloney's *Gentle Craft.*
The battle scenes are stirring and vivid, but highly
extravagant; the scenes of martyrdom are affected.
Both these series of incidents are important, however,
as they appertain to ancient traditions of the Gentle
Craft. The battle scenes, including Crispianus' noble
conduct in battle, and the religious element have already been discussed.

Like Dekker, Rowley is more skillful in depicting
shop scenes than in describing wild and improbable

[23] Dekker's *Shoemakers' Holiday.* Its position in the play has
not been found with certainty; it is sometimes given in Act 5,
sc. 4. This might be compared with Martin Parker's ballad, *The
Three merry Cobblers,* Roxburghe Ballad Socy., vol. 2, p. 586.
[24] C. W. Stork, *William Rowley.*

adventures. His art in *The Shoemaker a Gentleman* is in the realistic treatment of the various characters at their work as shoemakers, of their zest and joy in their work, and of the romantic plot which is skillfully interwoven with the shop scenes.

The sons of the British king, under the names of Crispinus and Crispianus become apprenticed to a shoemaker for a term of seven years. The shoemaker is a respectable, quiet man, with a great fondness for using (or just as often misusing) big words. His wife, Sisly, is a loud-spoken woman, a ruler of her husband, and, taken all in all, she is something of a scold. As in *The Shoemakers' Holiday,* so here also the shoemaker and his wife present certain contrasts to one another. With all her faults, however, she is a good worker. She spins the thread for the journeymen, Ralph and Barnaby. They jest and sing in the meantime. Sisly: "Thou seest I am at defiance with my worke till it be done, for I am alwaies spitting on my toe." She is probably here using her foot to fasten the thread.[25] The journeymen, Ralph and Barnaby, are glad to have Crispinus and Crispianus employed, as their fair faces will draw the custom of pretty wenches. An afternoon holiday is given in favor of the two new apprentices. The shoemaker expresses further his spirit of fellowship by saying:

> Provide dinner, Sis, Master, journimen, and Prentises,
> one table serves for all; wee feed as all fellowes.[26]

Crispinus and Barnaby go to the home of Leodice, the emperor's daughter, to fit her with shoes. She takes an interest in Crispinus, but hesitates to love

---

[25] Page 177, lines 11-12.   [26] Act 1, sc. 2, p. 183, line 185.

him on account of his low birth. At all events, she
pretends that her shoes do not fit, simply that she may
have a chance of seeing Crispinus again. Her nurse,
a figure like the nurse in *Romeo and Juliet*, tells her
that several of Leodice's own relatives were craftsmen.
This information satisfies her, and when Crispinus
reappears with her shoes she prepares to woo him.
She first pretends to find fault with him for courting
her nurse. Then, in what she pretends is a magic glass,
but which is only a mirror, she shows him his future
wife; i. e., herself. He tells her of his high birth, and
they agree to marry secretly the next day.[27]

Meanwhile, an officer comes to the shoemaker's
shop to press the journeymen and apprentices for war
against the Vandals. Barnaby pretends that he has
an ulcer about the heart, and is thus unfit for war,[28]
but the noble blood of Crispianus asserts itself, and
he is desirous of going to war. He goes, therefore,
greatly to the sorrow of the shoemaker's wife, who has
a great affection for him.

Crispinus, returning, gives a false excuse for his
lateness, saying that he stayed at court all night, fearing he would be drafted. The wife hits upon the real
cause of his tardiness, and scolds him for it. Her rage
increases when, later on, Crispinus tells her that his
wife is going to give birth to a child. There follows
a lively and humorous scene[29] in which the shoemaker

---

[27] Act 2, sc. 3. The scene is an excellent one.

[28] Barnaby's reflection on the advantages of remaining home
in safety resembles the famous soliloquy of Falstaff in *Henry IV*,
Part I, in which he claims that discretion is the better part
of valor.

[29] Act 4, sc. 1.

tries to appease his raging wife. On Crispinus' telling
her that he is of noble blood, she is quieted:

> I ever thought they were some worshipfull mans
> sonnes, they were such mannerly boys still.[30]

Sisly persuades them to set fire to the houses in the
neighborhood so that public attention may be engaged
while Leodice is brought secretly into her house.
Leodice gives birth to a boy, who, as Crispianus says,
shall

> plant a whole race of kings.
> Nor shall he scorne, till that race be runne,
> To call himself a Prince, yet a Shoemaker's sonne.[31]

The shoemakers in livery, with attendant music, usher
in the princess and her child. Barnaby's request that
the shoemakers may have a holiday each year on the
25th of October, is granted. Crispianus is made British
king in the South, Crispinus in the North. The latter
builds a church to St. Alban, the first British martyr.

The play is especially valuable, as before said, for
its realistic shop scenes, its careful attention to details
as to characters, tools, processes in the work of the
craft.[32] To a far greater extent than any play of the
period it introduces craftsmen's tools, such as stirrup,
awl, etc.[33] In its lively shop scenes and in its depiction
of fellowship and fraternity in the Hugh episode, and
in its realism, it compares well with Dekker's play.

The play can hardly be said to establish the valor
of shoemakers in battle, however. The shoemaker,

[30] Line 254, 5.   [31] Act 5, sc. 2.
[32] In this respect it resembles *The Shoemakers' Holiday.*
[33] A stirrup is an instrument used to put over the knee and
under the foot to hold work tight upon the knee.

enthusiastic over Crispianus' warlike exploits, which seem a credit to his craft, does not consider the fact that the bravery exhibited is by a prince, not by the genuine shoemaker, Barnaby, who is brave only in leading the shoemakers to fight with staves when he is fairly certain that no more fighting is needed.

These two plays on the Gentle Craft illustrate what excellent products issued when Deloney's tales were in large measure the sources. We may, therefore, truly regret the loss of several plays, perhaps as realistic and charming as these two, one at least of which is based partly on Deloney's *Thomas of Reading*. About 1596 Haughton, Day, and perhaps Samuel Rowley collaborated on *The Six Yeomen of the West*, a murder play.[34] Plays related to this one are the two parts of *The Six Clothiers of the West*, entered 1601. This was also a murder play, and was written by Haughton, Hathway, and Wentworth Smith. There is also the second part of *Tom Dough* by Day and Haughton. All of these characters appear in *Thomas of Reading; The Six Yeomen of the West* was based on part of Deloney's tale. Haughton's art in comedy and in realistic presentation of life is demonstrated in *Englishmen for my Money*. But that a play involving clothiers in which Haughton collaborated approaches the detail of the clothiers' craft to the extent to which Dekker or Rowley treat that of the shoemakers' craft, is doubtful, for Browne, a clothier, in *Englishmen for my Money* is not delineated with the least attention to his craft. Rawlins' *Rebellion*, 1637, roughly follows in outline Rowley's *Shoemaker a Gentleman* and is thus indirectly indebted to Deloney's novel.

[34] Yeomen here are clothiers.

Dekker's *Match me in London,* printed 1631, is a play somewhat difficult to classify. It presents none of the zest in labor so characteristic of the two shoemaker plays recently described; on the other hand, it pictures a tyrannical, lustful monarch, and his abduction of a craftsman's wife, thus utilizing a theme that became common. In its vivid presentation of shop scenes,[35] in its romantic love story, interwoven in a manner similar to the treatment of the Ralph-Jane plot, in its idealization of the shoemaker, Bilbo, and in its accurate delineation of him and Cordolente as shoemakers, it deserves a place here.

In Cordova there live two lovers, Cordolente and Tormiella. The latter's father has arranged that she marry another; so the lovers, accompanied by the witty and friendly shoemaker, Bilbo, escape to Seville. Here Cordolente opens a shop with miscellaneous wares, millinery, garters, gloves, and girdles. Bilbo is a salesman in the shop, but has not forgotten his old trade, for he says to the new apprentice, Lazarillo:

> there's not any Diego that treads
> upon Spanish leather, goes more upright upon
> the soles of his conscience than our master does.[36]

Out of regard for Cordolente, Bilbo says that he has left his trade, in which he had men-servants and maid-servants under him "to weare a flat cap here and cry what doe you lacke."

Tormiella works in the shop, embroidering muffs for ladies, and selling articles. The King, disguised as a citizen, together with a lady, enters the shop, ostensibly

---

[35] Vividness and detail are common to early and late plays on the crafts.
[36] Dekker's *Dramatic Works,* 1873 ed., vol. 4, Act 2, p. 150.

to buy a pair of gloves for a lady whom he claims has a hand the size of Tormiella's. Therefore he has her try on a pair of gloves. Bilbo's art as a salesman appears; he calls attention to the fine quality of the leather and the aroma of the gloves. There is a foreshadowing of the king's plot to abduct Tormiella in such expressions as:

BILBO. You shall have all the ware open'd i' the shop... but you shall be fitted.

KING. It needs not: that which is ope'd already shall serve my turne.[37]

Bilbo, trying to persuade them to buy certain articles which he claims are cheap for their quality, says:

"I assure your worship, my master will be a looser by you."[38] The King and lady lure Tormiella and the apprentice away, pretending that they want her to look at certain embroidery that they will employ her to work on. The apprentice is sent back to fetch a glove that the lady falsely says she dropped, and meanwhile Tormiella is abducted.

The King tries in vain to make her his mistress. She is the object of the Queen's jealousy and hatred, and has, on the whole, a wretched time at court.

Cordolente comes to court, boldly asks for his wife, and mentions the abuses and tyrannies of rulers. As he gains nothing by this method, he determines to use a stratagem, disguises himself as a shoemaker, and fits his wife with shoes. She pretends not to recognize him at first; he leads up to an introduction by desiring that she accept him again for her shoemaker, as formerly (i. e., he identifies the office of shoemaker

[37] Page 156.　　　　　　　　[38] Page 157.

with that of husband). He is a poor shopkeeper "whose ware is taken up by the king."[39]

TORM. Ile not change
Thee for a thousand Kings; there's gold.

CORD. I'me only taking instructions to make her a lower chopeene.[40] She finds fault that she's lifted too high.[41]

The king is finally persuaded to restore Tormiella to her husband.

Cobblers appear in a number of plays. Their business is mending, not making, shoes, and they are often considered botchers; i. e., clumsy workmen.[42] They are usually depicted in literature as cheerful and witty individuals; they are generally treated, especially in the early drama, with a sympathy kindred to that for the shoemakers. In *Julius Caesar* the cobbler is the only craftsman that has a ready wit and that puns on his craft. One source of the wit of cobblers lies in the fact that their tools and materials, as last, end, sole, awl, and mend have sounds that convey a physical and technical meaning and at the same time an abstract and general meaning. Such conditions readily lend themselves to puns.

Another play, in which Dekker collaborated with Haughton and Chettle, was *Patient Grissel*, 1600. It comprises the well known medieval story, and artfully contrasts Grissel's contentment as a helper to her

[39] Page 211.
[40] Chopeene is a high shoe worn by court ladies.
[41] The incident as a whole is somewhat reminiscent of the Ralph-Jane plot.
[42] For example, in Rowley's *Shoemaker a Gentleman* Barnaby explains the poor workmanship of Crispinus to Leodice by saying, "He's but a cobbler yet."

father, Janiculo, the country basket maker, with the sadness of her life at court. The famous lyric of Babulo, the witty clown and basket-maker, beginning "Art thou poor, yet hast thou golden slumbers, etc." is general in its praise of honest labor; no special attention is given in the play to basket-making.

Two plays of Dekker that present well the atmosphere of crafts are *If it be not good, the Devil is in it,* 1612; and *The Honest Whore,* Part I, 1604, and Part II, 1630, the end of Part I containing the famous words of Candido the linen-draper: "Christ the first true gentleman that ever breathed." Dekker and Middleton's *Roaring Girl* likewise contains vivid pictures of shop life.

Several plays deal with the craft of millers. *Faire Em, the Miller's Daughter of Manchester,* 1587,[43] is a play that deals with mill scenes. Fletcher and William Rowley's play, *The Maid in the Mill,* 1623, is worthy of some attention. It portrays realistically a miller (whose craft was a synonym for cheating and trickery from the Middle Ages) who nobly demands of the king his abducted daughter, Florimel.[44] The play is, therefore, a tribute to a despised craft, as Rawlins' *Rebellion* is to that of the tailors. In the house of her abductor, Count Otrante, Florimel sings songs which deal with her former trade. The following examples are almost in the spirit of Dekker's early plays.

[43] The ballad, *The Miller's Daughter of Manchester,* was perhaps the source of this play. There was a lost, undated play, *The King and Miller of Manchester,* referred to on page 124 of Ritson's *English Songs,* vol. 2.
[44] The behavior of Cordolente in *Match me in London* is similar.

Now having leisure, and a happy wind,
Thou mayst at pleasure cause the stones to grind;
Sails spread, and grist here ready to be ground;
Fy, stand not idly, but let the mill go round![45]

Shall the sails of my love stand still?
Shall the grist of my hopes be unground?
 Oh fy, oh fy, oh, fy!
Let the mill, let the mill go round![46]

A number of ballads deal with millers, often in a figurative way. *A Song*[47] is a late ballad that relates to the contentment of a miller, as a few lines of it will illustrate.

How happy the mortal
That lives by his mill;
That depends on his own,
Not on fortune's wheel.
. . . .
His mill goes clack, clack, clack,
How merrily, how merrily,
His mill goes clack.

The tinker is a stock figure in the literature of the period. He is often represented as a wanderer who makes more holes in a kettle than he mends. The following song is typical of tinkers:

Have you any work for a tinker, mistress?
Old brass, old pots, or kettles?
I'le mend them all with a tink, terry, tink,
And never hurt your mettles.[48]

The blacksmith is a figure celebrated in a number

[45] Act 5, sc. 2.   [46] Act 5, sc. 2.
[47] D'Urfey's *Pills to Purge Melancholy*, vol. 3, p. 125. *Jack Miller's Song* is another figurative ballad.
[48] *The Tinker*, from *Catch that Catch can*, 1667, Percy Socy. Pub., vol. 1, p. 155.

of ballads and songs.[49] One of the best portrayals of a blacksmith is that of Hodge in the play called *Thomas Lord Cromwell*, 1602. Hodge, a Putney blacksmith, travels to Italy with Cromwell. If the seas get rough, says Hodge, he will call on Vulcan, lord of the smiths, whose godhead will protect them. At Florence they are robbed of all their possessions. Hodge is about to take up his old trade, but expresses the hesitation of a local craftsman thus:

I am not acquainted with the humour of the horses in this country; whether they are not coltish, given much to kicking, or no; for when I have one leg in my hand, if he should up and lay t'other on my chaps, I were gone.[50]

The importance of such a utilitarian trade as his is stressed by Hodge; the rich or noble may at any time be reduced to want, but if trained to work at some trade, they may subsist anywhere.[51]

Four plays of interest that introduce the figure of the collier are Ulpian Fulwel's interlude, *Like Will to Like*, 1568; Richard Edwards' *Damon and Pithias*, 1571; *Grim the Collier of Croydon*, written about 1600; and Anthony Brewer's *Love-Sick King*, 1605. To a certain extent, these plays depict colliers consistently;

[49] For example, *The Blacksmith*, Percy Socy. Pub., vol. 1, p. 126; and *Who will be the smith's man?* Percy Socy., vol. 1, p. 152.

Other ballads, frequently hardly more than doggerel, that summarize the features of one or more crafts, are *The Merchant-Taylor's Song, The Conny Barber, The Brewer, London's ordinary,* and *The Jolly Tradesmen.*

[50] *Thomas Lord Cromwell*, A. F. Hopkinson edition, Act 3, sc. 1, p. 23.

[51] There is a similar observation in *The Four Prentices of London.*

blackened hands and faces associate the collier with
the devil.

The best portrait of a collier, and one that shows
him to best advantage as a citizen and craftsman is
in Brewer's *The Love-Sick King*, 1605, in the character
of Grim of Newcastle. His conduct in war has already
been mentioned. As director of seven hundred colliers
for the coal merchant, Randal, he encourages them,
telling them not to be ashamed to carry coals. Some
day he intends to be a lord, and all colliers under him
shall be ladies with black masks.

A feature of great interest is his pride in Newcastle
and its valuable product, coal. At first worried for
fear the Croydon colliers in rivalry will learn to make
charcoal out of wood, he soon assures everyone that
the superior excellence of Newcastle coal to that of
Croydon will be at once recognized. Having been
granted the position of the King's coal-carrier, he asks
that Newcastle colliers be placed above Croydon colliers.

This is a unique and important feature. There are
many instances of rivalry between allied crafts, but
none in drama so excellent as this of a craftsman's
civic pride in his work.

The drawer is another favorite figure in the drama.
As his name implies, his chief duty is to draw wine
and to supply guests with it.[52] This trade is well represented in Heywood's *Fair Maid of the West*, 1621 (?).
Clem, a drawer in the service of Besse, reflects his
trade in all of his actions. Indeed, in the long list of
craftsmen that Heywood presents in his plays, Clem

[52] Drawers or tapsters appear in Shakespeare's *Measure for
Measure*, Barry's *Ram Alley*, Nabbes' *Covent Garden*, etc.

is one of the very best portraits. He appears to good advantage as an artisan in the frequency with which he uses puns on his craft. In this respect he resembles the shoemakers, for like the tools of their craft, so the term "draw" may be extended to have several meanings. He says to Besse, who disguises herself as a man and wears a sword: "If you should swagger and kill anybody, I being a Vintner should be called to the Barre."[53] There is the following dialogue between him and the bully of the play:

CLEM.	If you lug me by the eares again, Ile draw.
ROUGHMAN.	Ha, what will you draw?
CLEM.	The best wine in the house.[54]

He will not remain on land, but accompanies his mistress on her naval expedition against the Spaniards:

No, it shall be seene that I who have beene brought up to draw wine, will see what water the ship drawes, or Ile beray the voyage... I doubt not but to prove an honour to all the Drawers in Cornwall.[55]

Clem's ready mention of the various wines testifies to his enthusiasm as a salesman:

What wine will you drinke? Claret, Metheglin, or Muskadine, Cyder or Pyrrey, to make you merry, Aragoosa, or Peter-see-mee, Canary or Charnico?[56]

He is daring, adventurous, proud and aspiring. He marches to the banquet and dances with the Moors.

[53] Heywood: *Dramatic Works,* 1874 ed., vol. 2, p. 284.
[54] Page 292. In Heywood's *Fortune by Land and Sea,* a drawer thinks that a man is slain, and exclaims: "They have drawn blood of this gentleman that I have drawn many a quart of wine to."
[55] Page 311.   [56] Page 301.
[57] Page 397.

Thinking that his mistress has been captured, he falls to his old trade again, and never discontinues talking about his pints and "pottles." "I am Clem of Foy, the Bashaw of Barbarie, who, from a Courtier of Fesse, am turned a Drawer in Florence."

A craft of some importance in the literature is that of the tailors. Proud of their title, "merchant-tailors," and of the fact that many kings and princes were free of the company,[58] the tailors enjoyed a certain eminence. Individual tailors are sometimes represented, however, who are mere botchers; i. e., poor workmen. In *The Weakest Goeth to the Wall*, 1600, is depicted a botcher, Barnabie Bunch, as a jolly and witty devotee of English ale. He is a contrast to the French tailor type in his national preferences. His trade was formerly that of an English ale-draper (an ale-house keeper), and he claims that in England, but not in France, a poor person can get ale for a penny. While at work with his shears, he complains about the bad smelling socks of the French. But his prevailing cheerfulness, singing while toiling, his reverence for the tailor's craft, and his promise to the apprentices, on being made sexton, not to ring the morning bell until it is past five (thus giving them an extra hour's sleep), remind us of the excellent early creations of Dekker.

Some of the leading satirical works on tailors are among the later ballads, such as *The Maidens Frollick*, in which six girls, disguised as seamen, press fourteen timid tailors for service.[59] In *An Answer to the Maidens*

---

[58] This is seen in their mayoralty shows and in *The Merchant Taylor's Song*, Evans' *Old Ballads*, vol. 3, p. 8.

[59] Roxburghe Ballad Socy., vol. 3, p. 402.

Frollick, one of the tailors says, on discovering the fraud:

> Calling my wife, she'd 'a ended the strife;
> But from my own part I ne'er fought in my life —
> I'm a tailor.

Another humorous ballad of this type is one called *A Dreadful Battle between a Taylor and a Louse,*[60] which tells how a tailor attacks a louse with all his weapons: needle, shears, etc., protecting himself with only a thimble. He finally conquers her and throws her into his "hell."[61]

Since tailors are fashioners and caterers to pride, they are at times represented as artistic. In the prologue to Lyly's *Midas,* 1592, are the words:

> Come to the taylor, hee is gone to the painters to learne how more cunning may lurke in the fashion, then can be expressed in the making.[62]

Taylor's *Prayse of the Needle,* printed in 1640, gives some realistic detail of the arts of sewing and embroidery.[63] They are glorified in the usual stereotyped ways by reference to their antiquity; their universal

[60] Roxburghe Ballad Socy., vol. 7, p. 466.
Ballads with somewhat similar themes are *A Leicestershire Frolic* and *Courageous Betty of Chick Lane.*

[61] "Hell" was the name given to a compartment under a tailor's table in which he threw stolen material from garments. Cf. Overbury's description of a tailor in *Characters* and Stephen's description of a tailor's man in *Essayes and Characters.*

[62] The same play goes into some treatment of the barber, Motto, as an artist who studies the court fashions. Cf. The conversation between Pennyboy, junior, and the fashioner in Jonson's *Staple of News,* act 1, sc. 2.

[63] Realism appears in the mention of a number of stitches and types of needle work.

and manifold use; by the fact that illustrious persons of past and present practiced the arts; and because the arts themselves are associated with beauty in their power to depict nature.

In *The Fair Maid of the Exchange,* 1607, perhaps by Thomas Heywood, there is a female apprentice, Phillis, who visits the shop of a pattern drawer with whom she is in love, and says that she wants him to do a piece of work in the following way:

> Onely this handkercher, a young gentlewoman,
> Wish'd me acquaint you with her mind herein:
> In one corner of the same, place wanton love,
> Drawing his bow shooting an amorous dart,
> Opposite against him an arrow in a heart,
> In a third corner, picture forth disdaine
> A cruell fate unto a loving vaine.
>
> In the fourth draw a springing Laurel tree
> Circled about with a ring of poesie: and thus it is:
> Love wounds the heart, and conquers fell disdaine,
> Love pitties love, seeing true love in paine:
> Love seeing Love, how faithfull Love did breath,
> At length impald Love with a Laurell wreath.[44]

There is a ballad of a certain literary merit that celebrates the dignified and ancient craft of weaving, ennobling it as an art rather than as a mere commercial pursuit. The ballad, whose opening lines are lost, gives the words of a father who is apprenticing his son to the weaver's craft. He mentions the ancient dignity of the craft; there is, moreover, practical value in having such an art at one's fingers' ends:

> For skill doth stay when goods be gone
> and riches all be spente.

[44] Heywood: *Dramatic Works,* vol. 2, 1874 ed., pp. 31, 32.

The father does not **fail to** observe that Minerva practiced the art.

> An arte whose end was never knowne,
> a curious[65] arte and fine,
> even such as Pallas, heavenly dame,
> did practice many a tyme.
> Therefore, to doe thy father's will
> thy paines do thou imploye
> so shalt thou be a commonwealth
> a member of great joy.[66]

Artistry in the goldsmith's craft is to be found in Drayton's Epistle, *Edward IV to Jane Shore*, in his *England's Heroical Epistles*, 1597. The story of Jane Shore is a very popular one, many works having been written about her.[67]

Jane Shore, wife of Matthew Shore, a citizen (and, according to Heywood's play, Drayton's poems, and the ballads, a goldsmith), prostitutes herself for King

[65] *Curious;* i. e., the art was one in which there was much to be learned, and much accuracy to be used.

[66] Shirburn Ballads, appendix IV.

[67] At least a dozen works besides the prose chronicles deal with it; and there are many references to it in historical and literary works. There is a poem on the subject by Thomas Churchyard in *Mirror for Magistrates*, one by Anthony Chute, and two by Michael Drayton in his *Heroical Epistles*. There are also a number of ballads on Jane Shore; and there are plays that introduce or refer to her, as the various plays on Richard III, as well as dramas in which she plays a conspicuous part, as *The Booke of Shoare, The Life and Death of Master Shoare*, 1599 (doubtless confused with Heywood's *King Edward IV*, in two parts, 1600),* a lost play of 1602 called *Jane Shore*, and Nicholas Rowe's *Jane Shore*, 1714.

* In *Pimlyco* is a reference to a play called *Shore* and its popularity.

[68] She married young. When the king tempted her, "the respect of his royaltie, the hope of gay apparel, ease, pleasure, and other wanton wealth, was able soone to perse a soft tender heart." — Hall: *Chronicle*, S. 363.

Edward IV. Her motive, brought out carefully in some accounts, is pride.[68] A concubine and person of much power, influence, and beneficence in the court during the king's lifetime, she is condemned by his successor, Richard III, to do public penance as a whore.

Drayton's Epistle is a combination of romance and realism, and may have been used by Heywood in his *King Edward IV*. It describes how King Edward IV comes disguised to see the famous Jane Shore in her husband's goldsmith shop in Lombard Street, London. Poetic and imaginative though the picture is, it gives the atmosphere of the goldsmith's shop excellently well. The craftsman's wife being in the shop is typical of many shops, especially as depicted in the literature of the 17th century. A handsome wife or daughter was not only a worker in the shop, but was also frequently exhibited by the master there, because she attracted customers. It became a rather frequent theme in the 17th century drama for the prodigal gallant to revenge himself on the deceptions of the craftsman by seducing his wife or daughter. So it is with this poem to some extent: the city meanness may be represented by the goldsmith, Matthew Shore, and the prodigal and lustful gallant may be typified in King Edward IV.

The king begrudges the city such a beauty as Jane Shore, greater than any in the court. In technical terms familiar to her through her knowledge of the jeweler's and goldsmith's craft, he presents his suit to her, flattering her beauty, and luring her by an appeal to her aspirations in such words as "kingly state."

> If now thy Beauty be of such Esteem,
> Which all of so rare Excellency deem?
> What would it be, and prized at what Rate,

Were it adorned with a Kingly State?
Which being now but in so mean a Bed,
Is like an un-cut Diamond in Lead,
E'er it be set in some high-prized Ring,
Or garnished with rich Enamelling;
We see the Beauty of the Stone is spilt,
Wanting the gracious Ornament of Gilt.["]

The king continues, giving a description of the gold-smith, whose quick eye has observed the king's interest in something in his shop:

Passing thy Shop, thy Husband call'd me back,
Demanding what rare Jewel I did lack,
I want (thought I) one that I dare not crave,
And one, I fear, thou wilt not let me have.
He calls for Caskets forth, and shews me store;
But yet I knew he had one Jewel more,
And deadly curs'd him, that he did deny it,
That I might not for Love or Money buy it.

The cook is an interesting figure in literature of the period. Sometimes he is represented as a tyrant in the kitchen, as in Thomas Nabbes' *Microcosmus*, 1637; at other times he is depicted as one having rare decorative talents. The cook in Fletcher's *Rollo*, 1624, and Furnace, the cook in Massinger's *New Way to Pay Old Debts*, 1632, are excellently delineated.

The most poetic and comprehensive description of a cook's craft, one that may have influenced later descriptions of cooks, is in Jonson's *Staple of News*, 1625. Lickfinger's description of his office, that of a cook, is almost worthy to compare with the treatment of shoemakers in Rowley's and Dekker's plays above described:

["] Lines 23-32.

A master-cook! why, he's the man of men,
For a professor! he designs, he draws,
He paints, he carves, he builds, he fortifies,
Makes citadels of curious fowl and fish,
Some he dry-dishes, some motes round with broths;
Mounts marrow-bones, cuts fifty-angled custards,
Rears bulwark pies, and for his outer works,
He raiseth ramparts of immortal crust;
And teacheth all the tactics, at one dinner:
What ranks, what files, to put his dishes in;
The whole art military. Then he knows
The influence of the stars upon his meats,
And all their seasons, tempers, qualities,
And so to fit his relishes and sauces.
He has nature in a pot, 'bove all the chymists,
Or airy brethren of the Rosie-cross.
He is an architect, an engineer,
A soldier, a physician, a philosopher,
A general mathematician.[70]

The opening part of *The Wisdom of Doctor Dodypoll,*
1600, has some excellent poetry on the art of painting.
Earl Lassingbergh, disguised as a painter, makes a
picture of his love, Lucilia, who reproves him for being
a mercenary painter. He replies that painting is an
art that approaches that of the creation of the world:

> the world
> With all her beautie was by painting made.
> Looke on the heavens colour'd with golden starres,
> The firmamentall ground of it all blew:
> Looke on the ayre where, with a hundred changes,
> The watry Rain-bow doth imbrace the earth:
> Looke on the summer fields adorned with flowers, —

[70] *The Works of Ben Jonson,* 1875 edition, vol. 5, Act 4, sc. 1,
p. 252. These lines are also found in Jonson's masque *Neptune's
Triumph.* The lines were taken from Posidippus's *Athenaeus.*

How much is natures painting honour'd there?
nature her selfe divine,
In all things she hath made is a meere Painter.[71]

An important feature of the artisan and his labor is in the work and trade songs. These frequently express a deep interest in the labor and give a vivid atmosphere to the scene. A number of the work songs have been discussed already.[72]

A song that is very vivid in its picture of the work in question is one from *Ralph Roister Doister;* Annot knits, Tibet sews and Madge spins on the distaff:

> Pipe Mery Annot, etc.,
> Trilla, Trilla, Trillarie,
> Worke Tibet, worke Annot, worke Margerie.
> Sewe Tibet, knitte Annot, spinne Margerie,
> Let us see who shall winne the victorie.
>
> Pipe merrie Annot, etc.,
> Trilla, Trilla, Trillarie,
> What Tibet, what Annot, what Margerie,
> Ye sleepe, but we doe not, that shall we trie.
> Your fingers be nombde, our worke will not lie.
>
> Pipe mery Annot, etc.,
> Trilla, Trilla, Trillarie,
> Nowe Tibet, nowe Annot, nowe Margerie,
> Nowe whippet apace for the maystrie,
> But it will not be, our mouth is so drie.[73]

[71] A. H. Bullen, *Old Plays*, vol. 3, p. 100.
St. Bonaventura, a 13th century Franciscan, compares the human artificer to the "Great Artificer." *De Reductione Artium ad Theologiam*, section 26.
[72] Those already discussed are the lyric in *Patient Grissel* beginning: "Art thou poor, yet hast thou golden slumbers;" the weavers' song in *Jack of Newbury;* and the journeymen shoemakers' poem about St. Hugh's bones in Deloney's *Gentle Craft.* Part 1.
[73] Act 1, sc. 3.

What could be more vivid as a description of tired and sleepy working girls, trying in vain to continue their work? The attempt to ward off sleep by singing and competing with one another is arrested by increasing drowsiness, naturally accompanied by numb fingers and dry mouths.

In any treatment of crafts and craftsmen, we are necessarily involved, to a certain extent, in a consideration also of trades. Traders on a small scale, such as peddlers and costermongers, frequently came from the ranks of the craftsmen, and manufactured some of their own wares.[74] Their trade cries contributed much to the noise and bustle of the street. The screaming of the fish-wives and oyster-wives became proverbial in the 16th and 17th centuries. Various works testify to the confusion caused by these tradesmen; e. g., Lydgate's *London Lickpeny*. This gives the atmosphere of several medieval trade centers: in Westminster were sold felt hats and spectacles for the dignified and learned lawyers and scholars; in Cheapside the mercers cried out their wares of velvet, silk, and lawn; in Canwick Street the drapers congregated. Jacobean works that represent trade scenes and cries are Jonson's *Silent Woman* and *Bartholomew Fair*.

Inasmuch as a thorough study of the trade cries is impossible here, attention will be given to some of the more literary selections, and the types of salesmanship that these represent. It must be understood that these rhymes were generally sung and not spoken; hence they had an additional attraction which is lost to the reader. Certain of the works to be considered re-

[74] C. Hindley's *History of the Cries of London* is a good guide for this study.

semble some of the preceding ones; but they vary from
them in stressing the products for sale rather than
the character of the craftsman or trader in question.
These early trade and work songs are seldom paralleled in the present day; although it is true that
factory hands and laborers often sing or whistle in
unison while at work, their songs seldom appertain
to the work in which they are engaged. The dealers
and merchants of today attempt to catch the prospective buyer's attention by some appeal to his desire
rather than by any exhibition of singing.[75] In the
depiction of tradesmen and artisans in Elizabethan
literature, on the other hand, we have trade songs extant; in certain cases the music of these has been
preserved. Some of the finer ones, when given by a
clear and musical voice, will catch the ear, just as a
beautifully decorated shop window will attract the eye.

Some trade songs deal with the selling of brooms;
e. g., in Wilson's *Three Ladies of London* Female Conscience tries to sell her brooms for old boots and shoes.
In the interesting medley called *The London Chanticleers*, Heath, the broomman, sings out his wares,
mentioning that it is necessary for women to keep

[75] There are, however, a few exceptions to this. Doubtless
the following trade song has often been observed during the
Christmas season:

"Holly wreaths, holly wreaths,
Come and buy your holly wreaths."

I have also observed the following song on one occasion:

"Ten a bunch for celery hearts,
All sweet celery hearts,
Ten a bunch."

their rooms clean in order to gain the good will of the fairies.

Two ballads that represent the praise of ale are *The Merry Hostess*[76] and *Good Ale for my Money.*[77] The first of these presents a very lively picture of a tavern in which are many customers composed of craftsmen, and a hostess who praises the ale that she sells.

Miscellaneous trade songs are typified very well in *The Traders Medley,*[78] *The Common Cries of London,*[79] and Heywood's verses called *The Cries of Rome.*[80]

One of the most poetic trade songs is in Oliphant's *Musa Madrigalesca.*[81]

> Fine knacks for ladies;
> Cheap, choice, nice and new.
> Good pennyworths but money cannot move;
> I keep a fair, but for the fair to view.
> A beggar may be liberal of love.
> Tho' all my wares be trash, my heart is true.

An interesting phase of this study is that which deals with the psychology of advertising. There have always been keen salesmen who know how to devise songs that have a universal appeal to customers. Still others rapidly read the various traits and desires of prospective customers and invent a song on the spur of the moment. There will follow, then, a few instances of the more poetic appeals to customers.

An instance is in the following words sung by

[76] Roxburghe Ballad Socy., vol. 3, p. 306.
[77] Roxburghe Ballads, vol. 2, p. 30.
[78] J. Ashton's *Century of Ballads*, p. 71.
[79] J. P. Collier's *Book of Roxburghe Ballads*, p. 207.
[80] They are at the end of his *Rape of Lucrece.*
[81] Page 165.

George, a mercer's young and outwardly attractive apprentice in Middleton's *Anything for a Quiet Life:*

> What is't you lack, you lack, you lack?
> Stuffs for the belly or the back?
> Silk grograns, satins, velvet fine,
> The rosy-colour'd carnadine,
> Your nutmeg hue, or gingerline,
> Cloth-of-tissue or tabine,
> That like beaten gold will shine
> In your amourous ladies' eyne,
> Whilst you their softer silks do twine?
> What is't you lack, you lack, you lack?[82]

This melodious passage illustrates good salesmanship. The young apprentice's vivid presentation of the wares and his artful suggestion of "amorous ladies" undoubtedly stimulated many customers.[83]

There are many songs that advertise clothing or certain personal decorations, and as a consequence are often associated with subtle flattery. For example, there is a trade song in G. Markham and W. Sampson's play, *Herod and Antipater.* The dealer in the song beginning *Come will you buy*— claims that he has gums that can puff out fallen cheeks, and mentions several preparations to protract youth, and to promote love and fruitfulness. *The Painter's Song of London*[84] describes a merchant who tries to sell paint to girls to give them a good complexion. A more interesting specimen of this type is *The Pedlar's Lamentation.*[85]

[82] Act 2, sc. 2, opening lines.
[83] In Act 1, sc. 3 of Massinger's *Renegado* Vitelle, acting as shopkeeper, advertises his china ware in poetic language. The passage has, however, less concreteness than the above passage of Middleton.
[84] Percy Socy. Pub., vol. 1, p. 152.
[85] Collier's *A Book of Roxburghe Ballads*, p. 304.

Here, the dealer exhibits his miscellaneous assortment
of wares which comprise dresses, hoods, coifes, laces,
gloves, perfumes, hair powders and song-books.

> I'll make you fine;
> Young Billy shall look as spruce as the day,
> And pretty sweet Betty more finer than May.

One of the most poetic and artful of trade songs
is that sung by Autolycus in Shakespeare's *Winter's
Tale.*[86]

> Lawn, as white as driven snow;
> Cyprus, black as e'er was crow;
> Gloves, as sweet as damask roses;
> Masks for faces, and for noses;
> Bugle-bracelet, necklace-amber,
> Perfume for a lady's chamber;
> Golden quoifs, and stomachers,
> For my lads to give their dears;
> Pins and poking-sticks of steel,
> What maids lack from head to heel:
> Come, buy of me, come; come buy, come buy;
> Buy, lads, or else your lasses cry;
> Come, buy, etc.

A branch of salesmanship that offers good opportunities for a keen merchant is the selling of ballads.
It is a subject that draws us somewhat away from a
study of craftsmen; but, since craftsmen, like many
people of slim education, are superstitious, they take
a deep interest in ballads that describe monstrosities,
such as Autolycus' one about a usurer's wife who "was
brought to bed of twenty money-bags at a burden."[87]
Craftsmen are especially interested in ballads that celebrate their own exploits, as the *Ballad of the London*

[86] Act 4, sc. 3.   [87] *Winter's Tale*, Act 4, sc. 3.

Prentice, exhibited by Ditty, the ballad dealer, in *The London Chanticleers*.[88]

One phase of the artisan and his work that is stressed in the 17th century literature deals with his cheating in trade. This treatment is not new with the 17th century; in the Middle Ages certain trades, such as the miller's[89] were especially open to criticism. In the early years of Elizabeth's reign some of the plays of Robert Wilson expose the abuses in trade; F. T's *Debate betweene Pride and Lowliness*, 1570, c.,[90] and Gascoigne's *Steel Glas*, 1576, are poems which do likewise. The last mentioned work anticipates a Utopia in the industrial and commercial world only when certain deceptions in trade are discontinued. Among other criticisms the author accuses cutlers of selling rusty blades and hiding cracks with solder; goldsmiths of using soldered crowns; upholsterers of selling feathers with dust; and pewterers of infecting tin with lead.[91]

The prose of the period frequently represents craftsmen as deceivers or as the victims of cheating. The jest-book is a form of popular prose that sometimes deals with artisans. In its commonest form the jest-book introduces a character who is invariably successful in any trick, however contemptible and stupid, that he plays on someone else, the victim usually being an extreme type of gull. We see this tendency of jesting in some of Deloney's characters, especially in the Green King, who is successful in a number of jests. A few

[88] The play is in Dodsley's *Old English Plays*, vol. 12. The passage referred to is in scene 3.
[89] Chaucer's reeve's tale of a miller is an illustration.
[90] This is the source of Greene's *Quip for an Upstart Courtier.*
[91] W. C. Hazlitt ed., vol. 2, pp. 211, 212.

of these tracts which lay emphasis on craftsmen are
*The Pleasant Conceites of Old Hobson the Merry
Londoner*, 1607,[92] *The Mad Pranks and Merry Jests
of Robin Goodfellow*, 1588; *Tarlton's Newes out of
Purgatory*,[93] on or before 1590; *Scoggin's Jests*, 1565;
Tarlton's Jests;[94] and *The Cozenages of the Wests*,
1613.[95] Two works somewhat like the jest-books are
The Tinker of Turvey, or *The Cobler of Canterbury*[96]
and *Westward for Smelts*, 1603.[97] Both of these works
are somewhat imitative of Chaucer's *Canterbury Tales*,
in that several characters tell stores appropriate to
their occupation and rank that picture rivalry between
different trades and crafts.

In the prose of Greene and Dekker are representations of artisans and traders who are either cheated
by professional sharpers or who are deceptive themselves. Greene's *Notable Discovery of Coosnage*, 1591-2,
and Dekker's *Jests to Make You Merry*, 1607, are instances of the former type.

One of the best illustrations of the craftsmen as
deceivers is Greene's *Quip for an Upstart Courtier*,
1592,[98] a prose work partly allegorical, partly humor-

[92] This work, which was published by Richard Johnson may
be found in Percy Socy. Pubs., vol. 9. In Heywood's *If You
Know Not Me, You Know Nobody* the same well known haberdasher appears but is delineated differently.

[93] Shakespeare Society, 1920.

[94] Shakespeare Socy., 19-20.

[95] Shakespeare Socy., 25-26. This work, which tells how Alice
West, a fortune teller, deceives many craftsmen, throws light
on the superstitions of the latter.

[96] *The Tinker of Turvey*, 1600, c., is a modification of an
earlier tract, *The Cobler of Caunterburie*, 1590.

[97] Percy Socy., vol. 21.

[98] The work may be found in Collier's *Miscellaneous Tracts*.
The source of Greene's work is F. T's *Debate betweene Pride
and Lowliness*.

ous, and partly realistic. Greene treats craftsmen as
mischievous sharpers in general, but in a somewhat
good-humored way, presenting them as sly rogues
rather than as malicious scoundrels. Nevertheless, this
study introduces representatives of some sixty crafts
(including all of the twelve great companies except
the salters and fishmongers) nearly all of whom are
accused of cheating, and their deceptive tricks are
described. The work also charges them with pride, a
trait to be later on censured by Dekker.

The story tells how, on a spring day, from opposite
directions there appear to a certain dreamer one in
fine velvet breeches and another in plain cloth ones.
The former, representing one of noble blood, claims
priority in England. Cloth-breeches, the English citizen,
however, claims a better right to it as representative
of "the old and worthie customs of the gentilitie and
yeomanrye of England," and a wearer of what his
forefathers wore before there was pride. To Velvet-
breeches' claim that he was called from Italy and
condescended to come into England, Cloth-breeches
replies :

Is an ancient honor tied to an outward bravery or not rather
true nobility, a minde excellently qualified with rare vertues?[99]

Velvet-breeches, he continues, is the refuse of Italy,
and is coming to degenerate England also.

A court session is arranged to decide it, Velvet-
breeches being plaintiff. The disputants wait now for
jurymen. One craftsman or tradesman appears after
another, their merits and vices are weighed while they
are considered for eligibility to the jury. In this way

[99] Page 16.

the deceits in the different trades are exposed. To take
an illustration, Velvet-breeches will not have a merchant, mercer, goldsmith, or draper, because each of
these is often a usurer. Criticisms of other craftsmen
follow. A tanner, shoemaker, and currier appear.
Cloth-breeches criticises the private gains of the tanner, a craftsman who is, for the most part, prosperous.
The tanner has many devices to make leather quickly,
but of poor quality. He uses fats wrongly in the treatment of hides. Instead of letting a hide lie for nine
months, he lets it lie only three months. Marle and
ashenbark are used to make the leather appear good,
but it is really no more lasting than paper. The tanner
cares nothing for others; he thinks mainly of marrying
his daughter to a rich esquire. The currier, continues
Cloth-breeches, is also bad. He uses mixed kitchen
stuff, instead of tallow. He buys leather pieces, calf
skins, etc., and sells them at too high a price to the
poor shoemaker, who must buy in small quantities.
Despite the fact that shoemakers are the victims of
more fortunate tanners and curriers, the latter sometimes are in league with a rascal shoemaker "that
neither respecteth God, the commonwealth, nor his
company."[100] Shoemakers often join a neat's leather
vamp to a calf's leather heel. A skinner, joiner, saddler, waterman, cutler, bellows-mender, plasterer, and
printer appear. Velvet-breeches approves of some of
them because he gets them to do superfluous work for
his clothes. Cloth-breeches, however, has a series of
accusations: the skinner takes a cheap skin, and
swears that it came from Muscovy or Calabria; the
saddler stuffs his pannels with straw; the joiner puts

[100] Page 46.

sap into the mortesels (i. e., mortices) ; the cutler cheats poor men. Cloth-breeches makes charges of one kind or another against nearly all craftsmen : the brick-layer makes chimneys that do not transmit smoke properly; the butcher, partly forced to cheat because the grazier charges him exorbitant sums for cattle, puts fresh blood on an old cow, and sells it for new; the brewer is far too sparing of his malt; the baker, whose chief interest is in making his daughter a gentle-woman, puts yeast and salt in the bread to make it heavy; tapsters and victuallers put much froth in their cans, and add more to the score than the customer ordered or received; vintners treat colorless wines with the strongly colored, and dilute the more expensive ones with the cheaper; cooks serve cheap and old meats; the tinker makes three holes where he mends one,[101] and is partly a highway robber; chandlers use dross over wicks and put tallow on the outside; haber-dashers trim up old felts to pass for new; grocers adulterate spices with dross and refuse; millers take double toll, and have false hoppers to convey away the meal.

The crafts that receive the largest amount of censure are several of the rich livery companies, especially those connected with the clothing industry, the mem-bers of which were, together with those of several other companies, guilty of usury. Velvet-breeches complains of the usury and extortion of goldsmiths as follows:

...they let young gentlemen have commodities of plate for ten in the hundred, but they must loose the fashion in sellinge

[101] The making of several holes while mending one was a proverbial charge against tinkers, as several of the ballads illustrate.

it againe ..... beside they are most of them skilde in alcumy, and can temper metals shrewdly,[102] with no little profite to themselves and disadvantage to the buier.[103]

The draper keeps such a dark shop that no man can choose a piece of cloth with accuracy.[104] He has the clothworker draw and stretch the cloth to make it seem large, a practice which weakens it. The clothworkers make cloth appear to have a fine nap by pressing and powdering it; they prove themselves the draper's ministers to execute his subtleties. Cloth-breeches then accuses the weavers of drawing out thread in such a way as to make it seem heavily woven, though it is really slenderly woven. They steal much yarn from poor country wives. Referring to the foreign customs introducing themselves into English dress at this time, Cloth-breeches says of a Dutch shoemaker and a French milliner that "they be of Velvet-breeches' acquaintance, upstarts as well as he, that have brought with them pride and abuses into England."[105] Their superfluities are spoken of; they take work from London handicraftsmen.

The various craftsmen conclude that Cloth-breeches is the better and more ancient of the two. He was a companion to kings, nobility, etc., whereas Velvet-

[102] Cf. Jonson's *The Alchemist.*

[103] Page 57, line 1. In *Eastward Hoe*, by Marston, Chapman, and Jonson, printed in 1605, Quicksilver, the goldsmith's wayward apprentice, though he has learned no industry from his trade, is familiar with deceptive devices of goldsmiths. He proposes to "blanche copper;" i. e., sublime it with arsenic, make it malleable and tenacious like silver, and then sell it for silver. He also intends to dissolve parts of angels in nitric acid and put dross on them in such a way that they shall recover their weight and shape.

[104] Cf. *Michaelmas Term.*

[105] Page 65, line 5.

breeches, begot of pride, and having come from Italy, is a raiser of rents and an enemy of the Commonwealth. A writer more Puritanical than Greene, and one who describes the deceptions of several crafts is Philip Stubbes. To testify partly that Stubbes and Greene were truthful in some of their accusations against craftsmen, mention might be made of some of the Elizabethan laws.[106] Statutes were directed against some of the stretching and drawing tricks of weavers and tuckers.

In Stubbes' *Anatomy of Abuses*, Part 2, 1583, he presents in the form of a dialogue complaints against various crafts and trades. There is here, then, much similarity to what has already been said about Greene's work. Deceits of miscellaneous crafts are exposed; those of fashioners, such as tailors, are harshly criticised as they are in the work of Greene, Rich,[107] and Dekker.

Stubbes departs for once from this stereotyped registering of vices in his humorous description of barbers. These are necessary, for men look beastly with long unkempt hair. With their several cuts, the Italian, French, and Spanish, they can make customers look handsome or terrible. They twirl mustaches from one ear to the other. Lathering is graphically described. The customer is perfumed, sprinkled with fragrant waters, and entertained by music. The extreme politeness of barbers is also mentioned.

Dekker's *Worke for Armorours*, 1609, an allegory that throws light on the industrial and social evils of the age, is sympathetic with the poorer crafts, but

[106] New Shakespeare Socy., Series 6, 12, page XIV.
[107] Barnaby Rich: *The Honesty of this age*, 1614.

hostile to the richer ones, such as the mercers and
goldsmiths. Cheating in trades is well represented in
Dekker's *Seven Deadly Sins of London*, 1606, and
Newes from Hell, 1606.

Ballads that represent deceptions in trade are *The
miller and his Sons*," "*Merry Tom of all Trades*," "*True
Blew the Plowman*," "*Robin Conscience*," "*Poor Robins
Dream*," and "*Death's Dance*."

One of the traits of craftsmen and their families is
pride. This is not slighted in literature; we see some
of it in Simon of Southampton's wife,[108] but there is
more of this treatment in 17th century literature. Nash,
Greene, Dekker, Stubbes, Rich, Rowlands, and Taylor
frequently hold pride up to ridicule. Thomas Nash,
with all his humor and vivacity, is at times Puritanical
and harsh in his characterization. In his "Pierce
Pennilesse," 1592, he pictures the excessively proud
artisans and merchants,[109] some of whom work themselves by flattery into the good graces of noblemen. In
his *Christ's Tears over Jerusalem*, 1593, there is disdain
of the citizen for the countryman, and of one craft
for a lower; e. g., the shoemaker for the cobbler, and
the cobbler for the carman.[110] Nash criticises strongly
the use of face paints and powders by women, and
their style of dress. In Stubbes' *Anatomy of Abuses*,[111]
the writer is not only opposed to pride in dress, but is
also opposed to the attending of shows and the playing
of dice or cards. Henry Crosse's *Vertues Common-*

---

[108]   Deloney's *Thomas of Reading*.
[109]   Collier ed., p. 2.
[110]   McKerrow ed., vol. 1, p. 135.
[111]   Part 1, New Shakespeare Socy., Series 6, 6.

wealth,[112] 1603, parallels some of the accusations of Stubbes in regard to counterfeit gentility.

In some of the works of Greene, Dekker, and Rich, where the element of pride is stressed, it is largely fostered by the constant changing of fashions on the part of tailors, mercers and barbers. Greene, in his *Defence of Conny-catching*,[113] combines the tailor's catering to pride with his deception in trade. He changes the style each week, and takes advantage of the fact that he is supplied with the material for clothing; for, owing to the changing styles, foolish customers do not know how much velvet to send. The tailor asks for more material than is needed for the suit and steals the remainder. The relation of tailors to pride in their introduction of new fashions is seen in the following works of Dekker: *Newes from Hell, A Knight's Conjuring, The Gull's Hornbook, Lanthorne and Candle-Light, A Strange Horse Race,* and *The Divels Last Will and Testament.*" In the last named work, which is allegorical, Hypocrisie is represented as being bound to a Puritan tailor, and making with him nothing but cloaks of religion of a thousand colors. Dekker anticipates here the ridicule of Puritanical hypocrisy in the Cavalier period. We shall see then how Puritans have Biblical texts embroidered on their garments. The dramatists especially ridicule Puritan women, who were mainly of the middle classes, and whose trades dealt especially with the fashions and sports that they themselves condemn. They were starchers, bugle-makers, tire-women, feather-makers,

[112] Grosart's *Occasional Issues*, vol. 7.
[113] Grosart ed., vol. 11.

confect-makers, and French fashioners.[114] Barnaby
Rich's *Honesty of this Age*, 1614,[115] and Samuel Rowlands' *Martin Markall*, 1610, in their enumeration of
several useless trades, carry on the criticism of tailors
as caterers to pride.

Taylor's *The World runnes on Wheels*[116] is an interesting instance of rivalry between crafts. There is
emphasized the evil effect that the introduction of
coaches has on the watermen's trade[117] and several of
the others; e. g., the ancient and profitable trade of
wheelwrights.[118]

A most excellent illustration of the artisan's cheating
in trade combined with his pride and hatred of the
high born classes is Middleton's play, *Michaelmas
Term*, 1607.[119] It embodies several disagreeable aspects
of the craftsman: cheating devices, usury, keen insight
into customers, materialism, indifference to any family
ties, suspicion in regard to his wife, love of worldly
honor, wealth, and lands, desire to gain the wonder
and the envy of fellow-craftsmen less fortunate.

The figure of chief interest is Quomodo, a prosperous
woolen-draper who darkens his shop and attributes the

[114] Randolph's *The Muse's Looking Glass* gives a good picture
of a Puritan feather-maker.

[115] Percy Socy. Pub., vol. 11.

[116] Printed in 1630.

[117] Watermen did not form a craft, but they composed an
organization which, as we shall see, aspired to social eminence
in a manner somewhat similar to that of craftsmen. Most of
Taylor's works here referred to are in Spenser Socy. Pub., vol. 2
to vol. 4.

[118] The wheelwrights made carts.

[119] The element of rivalry between the highborn and the low-
born is especially characteristic of Massinger's *New Way to Pay
Old Debts*.

condition to the weather.[120] His two attendants and accomplices are Shortyard and Falselight, their names being suggestive of their characteristics. His trust in the deviltry of these decoys is expressed thus:

> Go, make my coarse commodities look sleek;
> With subtle art beguile the honest eye.[121]

Together with Gum, the mercer, and Profit, the goldsmith, Quomodo, the draper, is represented as a usurer. His usury as a means of obtaining possession of the lands or estates of others is the chief source of interest in the play. He looks longingly at the land of a certain gallant, Easy, who, wishing ready money with which to defray the expense of a banquet with his friends, tries to borrow money from Quomodo.[122] The latter, declaring that he has no money at hand, offers Easy a commodity of cloth, something which bankrupt gallants frequently received and tried to sell quickly. Shortyard acts as a decoy, and pretends to Easy that he himself is in debt, and that his name is Blastfield. Shortyard pretends that he, also, is trying to borrow money from Quomodo; and Easy is thus led to take up this commodity of cloth with Shortyard. Quomodo artfully leads up to a suggestion that Easy be one of the signers of the bond by politely insinuating that

[120] Act 2, Scene 3. Dishonest tradesmen's darkening their shops is a practice alluded to at times. Cf. Brome's *City Wit*, Act 1, Scene 1.

[121] Dyce ed., vol. 1, p. 421.
Another play that is excellent in its presentation of the various deceits of tradesmen is Jonson's *Bartholomew Fair*, 1614.

[122] We have here a situation somewhat like that in *The Merchant of Venice*. A prodigal is in need of ready money from a close-fisted usurer, who knows how to take his advantage over his borrower's helplessness.

Easy has no substance. The gallant's pride, which Quomodo has been constantly observing, leads him to say positively that he has land and wealth, and signs the bond to prove it:[123]

> Master John Blastfield esquire, i' the wold of Kent: and Master Richard Easy, of Essex, gentleman, both bound to Ephestian Quomodo, citizen and draper of London; the sum, two hundred pound.

Falselight, the other accomplice, appearing as a young man needing ready substance with which to start business, pays sixty pounds for Easy's two hundred pounds' worth of cloth. The time being past when Easy had promised to pay for the cloth, he is arrested on Quomodo's suit by Shortyard and Falselight, who are disguised as sergeant and yeoman.

The yearning for land and estates on the part of craftsmen is well typified in Quomodo's joy on reflecting that Easy's land of Essex will be his:

> The land's mine; that's sure enough, boy, now shall I be divulg'd a landed man throughout the livery; one points, another whispers, a third frets inwardly; let him fret and hang! Especially his envy I shall have that would be fain, yet cannot be a knave, like an old lecher[124] girt in a furr'd gown, whose mind stands stiff, but his performance down. Now come my golden days in. Whither is worshipful Master Quomodo and his fair bedfellow rid forth? To his land in Essex whence come those goodly loads of logs? From his land in Essex. Where grows this pleasant fruit, says one citizen's wife in the row? At Master Quomodo's orchard in Essex. O, O, does it so? I thank you for that good news, i' faith.[125]

> A fine journey in the Whitsun holydays, i'faith, to ride down

[123] Act 2, sc. 3. [124] Lecher — leather.
[125] Act 3, sc. 4, p. 475.

with a number of citizens and their wives, some upon pillions, some upon side-saddles, I and little Thomasine i' th' middle, our son and heir, Sim Quomodo in a beach-colour taffeta jacket, some horse-length, or a long yard before us,[126] — there will be a fine show on's, I can tell you.

Easy is brought into Quomodo's shop and is confronted by the prospect of imprisonment unless someone will stand bail for Easy on a single bond of "body, goods, and lands, immediately before Master Quomodo."

Successful though Quomodo is thus far, he is eventually outwitted himself by a conspiracy of Thomasine, his wife, Easy, and his own accomplices.

Not only in this play which so darkly presents city life, but also in many others of this period are illustrations of the way in which fashioners, such as goldsmiths, mercers, and tailors, cater to the whims and desires of stylish gallants. In Marmion's *Fine Companion*, 1633,[127] various craftsmen; e. g., tailors, sempsters, and haberdashers cater to the interest of Careless, the "fine companion", in new clothes and in new toys. Most politely do they flatter him and suggest new styles.

Barbers are frequently introduced into plays. Associated with the Barber Surgeon's Guild, they had the privilege not only of cutting hair but also of letting blood and extracting teeth. The plays frequently represent them as cheats and as pretenders to greater surgical skill than they had. In Marston's *Dutch*

[126] Act 4, sc. 1, p. 490. There is a situation similar to this in Middleton's *Trick to Catch the Old One*. In this play, Hoard, a citizen, anticipates marrying a rich widow and riding to her lands.
[127] It is in Thomas White's *Old English Drama*, vol. 4. The reference is to Act 1, sc. 4.

Courtesan one who acts as a barber blinds his customer with soap, and then steals his money bag. In Beaumont and Fletcher's *Knight of the Burning Pestle,* in Middleton's *Anything for a Quiet Life,* and in the anonymous play, *A Knave in Graine,* are represented the barbers' double occupation of haircutting and surgery, especially in connection with the treatment of venereal diseases.[128] Barbers, as well as mercers, tailors, and other fashioners, are frequently depicted as extravagant in their encouragement of foreign fashions.

The element of pride in the artisan and his family is an interesting feature that will be stressed, somewhat apart from their work, in the next chapter.

[128] Quack surgery and aspirations of the unlearned to practice medicine and surgery are well represented in the following passage:

"In the time of Henry VIII, there was a great rabblement there, that took upon them to be surgeons. Some were sowgelders, with tinkers and coblers. ..... In two dressings they did commonly make their cures whole and sound for ever, so that they neither felt heat nor cold, nor no manner of pain after."

From J. Halle's *An Historiall Expostulation,* 1565. Percy Society, vol. 11.

CHAPTER IV

SOCIAL ASPIRATIONS OF THE ARTISAN

Something has already been said incidentally about the way in which artisans love to exhibit themselves in fashionable clothing, or in processions, such as the Lord Mayor's Show. The catering on the part of fashioners to pride in customers was also discussed. French and Spanish tailors are especially unpopular, not only because they cater to pride, but also because they put many English artisans out of work.

> They brought in fashions strange and new
> with golden garments bright:
> The farthingale, and mighty cuffes,
> with gownes of rare delight.
> Our London dames in Spanish pride
> did flourish everywhere.[1]

The master craftsman as a social climber has been discussed in the passage dealing with Middleton's *Michaelmas Term;* something remains to be said about the aspirations of the artisan's wife or daughter or apprentice, as this is a favorite theme in 17th century popular literature, especially the drama. Writers like Beaumont and Fletcher mercilessly satirize pride in

[1] From *The Lamentable Fall of Queen Elnor*, Roxburghe Ballads, vol. 2, p. 362.

During the apparent period of this ballad, the late 16th century, there was much rivalry between England and Spain. The story is also in Peele's *Edward I.*

the artisan class; Ben Jonson and his collaborator, Marston,[2] do likewise. Middleton carries on the realistic and satirical depiction of craftsmen and craftswomen as apes of the nobility, and influences some of Dekker's later plays in this respect. Disciples of Jonson, such as Brome, Cartwright, Randolph, Field, Marmion, Mayne, Glapthorne and Nabbes carry on his tradition, in this respect frequently repeating him or one another.[3] Some of these stock figures of the artisan class, as the apprentice or the craftswoman, occur also in the plays of miscellaneous writers, such as Cooke, Massinger, Ford, Tatham, and Shirley. Apprentices appear in some of the plays of Brome and especially of Shirley. In the plays of these later writers they are portrayed differently from the way in which 16th century writers portray them.

The artisan's imitation of the nobility is manifested in one or more of the following ways: copying of words, expressions, or gestures of noblemen, wearing attire like that worn in court, intermarrying with knights or earls, trying to obtain possession of lordly manors or estates. The yearning for land is a trait particularly conspicuous in the figure of Quomodo. Some of the childish forms of imitation, however, remain to be considered first.

Marston's *Dutch Courtesan*, 1605, affords a good illustration of a vintner's ambitious wife who has squires, gentlemen, and knights at her table to dine. Ashamed of the fact that her husband is a craftsman,

[2] Marston, Chapman, and Jonson collaborated in *Eastward Hoe*.

[3] For example, Cartwright's *Ordinary* and Mayne's *City Match* are rough copies of Jonson's *Alchemist* and *Silent Woman* respectively.

she has things spread handsomely, so as to disguise her bringing up.[4]

> I was a gentlewoman by my sister's side — I can tell ye so methodically. Methodically! I wonder where I got that word? O! Sir Aminadab Ruth bad me kiss him methodically! I had it somewhere, and I had it indeed.[5]

In Middleton's *Chaste Maid in Cheapside*, 1630, is the family of Yellowhammer, a goldsmith. The parents are desirous of marrying their son, Tim, and daughter, Moll, to wealth and renown. The former is thus sent to Cambridge, where he learns Latin, and the latter is taught dancing. The parents are unsuccessful in marrying their daughter as they wish to; but they succeed in marrying their son to a Welsh knight's niece, their object being to gain eminence and exhibit a seemingly learned young couple: Tim with his Latin quotations and his wife with her Welsh language. As such plays frequently develop, however, Tim finds that he has married a woman of a shady past and limited fortune.

Mistress Quickly in Shakespeare's *Henry IV*, Part 2, 1597-9, hostess of a tavern in Eastcheap, is an instance of one from the ranks of the artisans who imitates the words and gestures of the nobility. A source of the humor in the play is to be seen in her misuse and confusion of words; e. g., using "confirmities" for "infirmities".[6] Indeed, Shakespeare's depiction of imi-

---

[4] Pinnacia Stuff, in Jonson's *New Inn*, is a gaudily dressed tailor's wife, ashamed to be considered the wife of an artisan. This behavior is like that of the family in Brieux's *Three Daughters of M. Dupont*.

[5] Act 3, sc. 2.

[6] Act 2, sc. 4.

tative and childish traits among artisans is as excellent as is that of any of the other dramatists. The love that citizens (as portrayed in literature) have for association with royalty or knighthood is frequently an important governing motive in their actions. Hence, Mistress Quickly is persuaded by Falstaff, the knight, to withdraw the lawsuit which she had against him on account of his debts. Falstaff's tact is observable in the fact that he works on some of her characteristics that are typical of the citizen class, and flatters her very courteously. She bears in mind the important fact that this knight had promised to marry her and make her his lady. He had told her on the same day not to talk to Goodwife Keech, the butcher's wife, nor to such poor people, for before long she would be called "Madam."[7]

The development of the city woman in 16th and 17th century literature may be studied by considering a few miscellaneous works in which she appears. The wife of the craftsman from medieval times to 1600 is often represented as a valuable assistant to her husband in his work, or as an ardent worker in some other craft apart from his. Thus she is represented in several ballads; e. g., the medieval *How a Merchande dyd hys Wyfe Betray;* and Elizabethan parallels: *Penny-wise, pound-foolish*, 1631; *The Penny-worth of Wit*, 1560 c., and *The Chapman of a Pennyworthe of Wit*. In Deloney's fiction the wife is frequently represented as the superior of her husband in intellect and initiative, and as an excellent fellow-worker; e. g., the wife of Simon Eyre. Exceptions, however, which have been already pointed out, exist in the literature

---

[7] *Henry IV*, Part 2, Act 2, sc. 1.

even of medieval times, a period in which the wife's subservience to her husband was strongly insisted on. In Chaucer's *Prologue* to *The Canterbury Tales*, the wives of the successful artisans are represented as proud of the social eminence that their husbands' prosperity brings them. In Chaucer's remarkable portrait of the Wife of Bath he depicts a very individualized clothmaker who alone represents several aspects of the craftsman's wife as she appears in the literature of the period from 1557-1642, an age of individualism as contrasted with medieval emphasis on institutions. This Wife of Bath has excellent skill in her trade of cloth-making, as several of the craftsmen's wives in Deloney's, Dekker's, and Rowley's literature have skill in their trades. She has also the yearning for social eminence and prestige, as depicted in some of the craftsmen's wives in Stubbes' *Anatomy of Abuses*, in Deloney's fiction, and in the plays of Dekker, Jonson, Marston, Middleton, Massinger, and others. Chaucer's Wife of Bath has still another trait that appears in the later drama (most of which appears long after the death of Elizabeth) : she desires sovereignty over her husband.[8]

Coming to our period, we have several well delineated craftsmen's wives in Deloney's fiction; e. g., the industrious and enterprising wife of Simon Eyre, before commented upon. Far though Deloney is from being a satirist of artisans, he depicts in *Thomas of Reading* several vain city wives. These accomplish nothing that is worth while, but in their desire to

[8] Excellent discussions of the Wife of Bath are in G. L. Kittredge's *Chaucer's Discussion of Marriage*, in *Modern Philology*, April, 1912; and in W. W. Lawrence's *Marriage Group in 'The Canterbury Tales,'* in *Modern Philology*, Oct., 1913.

travel to London, and to dress gaily as craftsmen's wives do there, they anticipate a type common in Jacobean literature. The wives of Simon and Sutton prevail on their husbands to let them go to London, Simon's wife claiming that a woman should not be cooped up, but should enjoy the greatest pleasure, which is to see the fashions and manners of unknown places. The London merchants and their wives are hospitable to them; but the fine clothes of these women excite the envy of the clothiers' wives, "and grieved their hearts they had not the like."[9] Simon's wife sees no reason why the country dames, who are as beautiful as the city wives, and whose husbands are as rich as the Londoners, do not dress as well as the London merchants' wives. She tries to persuade her husband to give her London apparel.[10] She pretends, moreover, that she is sick and about to die, and that her cure will be effected only if she is given London clothes. Her husband finally gives in; she is provided with fine Cheapside gowns, being content with no other kind. The rest of the clothiers' wives follow her example, so that ever since, according to the story, "the wives of Southampton, Salisbury, Gloucester, Worcester, and Reading, went all as gallant and as brave as any Londoners' wives."[11] It is apparent that Deloney, writing as early as the last four years of the 16th century, had studied enough of the pride of craftsmen and merchants and their wives to anticipate some of the later portraits of artisans and citizens by Jonson,

[9] Aldrich and Kirtland ed., Chap. 6, p. 65.

[10] Chap. 6, p. 74. In Dekker's *Batchelor's Banquet* is another such wheedling wife.

[11] Ibid., p. 78.

Middleton, and Massinger. Simon's wife not being satisfied with a fine gown unless it is of an especially stylish type, a Cheapside gown, is paralleled in Massinger's portrait of a city wife who not only wants a coach, but also one drawn by four Flanders mares.[12]

Interesting portrayals of craftsmen's wives are seen in Rowley's *Shoemaker a Gentleman*, 1609; and in Dekker's *Shoemakers' Holiday*, 1599. In the former play, Sisley, the shoemaker's wife, is an industrious and skillful assistant to her husband in his work. Shrewish and overbearing though she is, the contrast to her meek husband, she does at no time express dissatisfaction with her low station in life. In Dekker's play, though an earlier one than Rowley's, there is presented a somewhat later stage of development of the craftsman's wife. After Eyre, the shoemaker, puts on his alderman's gown, his wife, Margery, realizes that she must now dress according to her high social station and get a French hood.

Marston, Chapman, and Jonson's *Eastward Hoe*, printed in 1605, is an extremely important member of a group of partially domestic plays in which craftsmen are introduced.

Touchstone, a goldsmith, has two apprentices: Golding, an industrious one; and Quicksilver, a lazy and wayward one. He has a wife who is at times industrious in the shop, but who is carried away by a desire for pomp and social eminence. This last tendency of hers is inherited in extreme degree by one of her daughters, Gertrude. Gertrude shuns her parents and their industry, will have nothing more to do with

[12] *The City Madam*, 1632.

Chittizens,[13] and imitates the fashions of the court.
She wears French and Scottish fashions in dress, and
wants to be a "lady" and ride in a coach. Imitating
still further the fashions of a lady, she reads chivalric
romances. After she obtains temporary possession of
a coach, her favorite expression becomes: "as I am
a Lady." Clever characterization on the part of the
dramatists may be seen in this last expression. It is
the custom of artisans, as they are presented in literature, to use such exclamations as the following: "As
God shall mend me," "As true as I live,"[14] and "As I
am a true woman."[15] Gertrude's "As I am a Lady"
is thus merely a modification of this custom of artisans,
a change of a word or two, as "woman" for "lady."
This shows that Gertrude, advanced socially as she sup-
poses, unconsciously reveals the traits of the humbler
classes from which she originated.

Quicksilver, the wayward apprentice, is similar to
Gertrude in some respects. He wears fine clothes,
carries a sword, dwells on the fact that his mother
was a gentlewoman, and quotes from the popular and
spectacular plays of the period, *The Spanish Tragedy*
and *Tamburlaine.* After being discharged from the
goldsmith's service because of laziness, he conspires
with Security, a usurer, to obtain the inherited land
of Gertrude. As subtle and cunning as a gallant, Quicksilver knows just where to appeal to Gertrude, and

[13] *Chittizens,* i. e., citizens. Cf. in Marston's *What you Will,*
1607, Celia, the daughter of a merchant.

[14] *Henry IV,* Part 1, Act 3, sc. 1. Hotspur tells his wife,
Kate, to leave off such expressions as these, for they sound like
oaths from the "base artisans."

[15] *Henry IV,* Part 2, Act 3, sc. 3. Mistress Quickly says
these words.

persuades her with the promise of a fine new gown to sign a deed giving over her land.

Sir Petronel, who passes for a knight, agrees to marry Gertrude and take her to his castle. She is easily persuaded to ride in a coach (the object of her heart's desire) to her knight's castle. She is doomed to disappointment, however, for the supposed knight is on another adventure. She soon realizes that her knight and his famous castle are imaginary, and wails over the decay of chivalry.[16] She is so hard pressed that she is even willing to sell her ladyship, and returns to her father, the goldsmith, who receives her reluctantly.

Meanwhile, Quicksilver and Petronel have wild schemes about taking a trip to Virginia on a search for gold. Quicksilver steals articles from Touchstone, the goldsmith, in order that they may be provided for the voyage. They squander their money, are shipwrecked, and later arrested. In prison Quicksilver recites the ballad of Mannington whose fall resembles his own. Golding, the industrious apprentice and former fellow of Quicksilver's, now an alderman's deputy, is the magistrate over the two prodigals, but acts leniently, and soon releases them. The play concludes with a general reconciliation.

Certain works of a similar nature but more tragic in outcome may be briefly considered. *A Warning for*

[16] Cf. a story by Rowlands in *Good News and Bad News*, 1622. A citizen's wife marries a knight in order to become "madam'd, worship'd, ladifide," and to ride in a coach. Her knight getting in debt, she is reduced to beggary.

Cf. the ballads, *The Slowmen of London*, D'Urfey's *Pills*, vol. 6, p. 93; and *Perkin in a Coal Sack*, in which a collier's wife desires a coach. D'Urfey's *Pills*, vol. 6, p. 254.

Faire Women, 1599,[17] is one of several domestic trage-
dies concerned with craftsmen. Anne Saunders, the
heroine and wife of the merchant-tailor, is the typically
ambitious wife of an artisan.

Anne desires more money for fine clothing than her
husband is willing to give. Mistress Drury, a fortune-
teller, takes advantage of Anne's anger at her husband;
and working on her superstitions, prophesies that she
will be a widow and a happy one:

> A gentleman, my girl, must be the next,
> A gallant fellow, one that is beloved,
> Of great estates, 'Tis plainly figured here,[18]
> And this is called, the Ladder of Promotion.
> .... the next
> Shall keep you in your hood and gown of silk,
> And when you stir abroad ride in your coach,
> And have your dozen men all in a livery,
> To wait upon you.[19]

Fascinated by this vivid prophecy, and soothed into
thinking that fate absolves human responsibility, Anne
comes to believe that it is God's will that her husband
must die, and, therefore, has she not a right to profit
by it? She is now ready to condone the murder of her
husband by Captain Browne, her paramour. She is
executed, together with him and his accomplices.

The story of Jane Shore, as it is given in Part 1
of Heywood's *King Edward IV,* printed in 1600,[20]
might also be called appropriately *A Warning for Fair
Women.* It is concerned not only with a fair woman,

[17] R. Simpson's *School of Shakespeare,* vol. 2.
[18] Lines 635-638.
[19] Lines 649-653.
[20] It is in volume 1 of the 1874 edition of Heywood's works.

but also with a fair woman who works in her husband's shop. This situation is a favorite one with the later dramatists, who often show the way in which this frequently builds up a craftsman's trade by attracting customers to his shop, and how it also often results in licentiousness and marital infidelity.[21] This play represents both results of the attractive wife used partly as a worker and partly as a fascinating ornament in the shop.

The theme, which has been considered before, deals with Jane Shore, the wife of Matthew Shore, a goldsmith, her amours with King Edward IV, her power in court, and her downfall and disgrace after the latter's death. It will not be treated fully here; but something will be said about Jane's waiting on the king, who poses as a customer;[22] inasmuch as there is interweaving of the details of the craft with the romantic story.[23]

King Edward IV, dressed as an ordinary man, enters

[21] Instances are in Middleton's *Family of Love* and Field's *Amends for Ladies*, printed in 1618. In the latter play Seldom and his beautiful wife work in a shop. The wife is subjected to many temptations. An allusion to the purpose of the fair wife in the shop is in the words of Lord Proudly to Seldom:
"Did not I set thee up,
Having no stock but thy shop and fair wife?"
Act 4, sc. 3.
"... thy shops with pretty wenches swarm,
Which for thy custome are a kinde of charme
To idle gallants."
From *Pasquils Palinodia*, 1619.
Grosart's *Occasional Issues*, vol. 5, p. 141.

[22] Heywood owes something here to Drayton's treatment of the theme in *Edward IV to Jane Shore*, one of his *Heroical Epistles*, 1597.

[23] As has been said before, there are few such cases outside of the novels of Deloney, and some of the plays of Dekker.

the shop, describing to himself Jane's beauty in terms
of jewels, such as diamonds, the description being
suggested by the jewelry in the shop.

JANE.   What would you buy, sir, that you look on here?
KING.   Your fairest jewel, be it not too dear.
        First how this sapphire, Mistress, that
        you wear?
        . . . .
JANE.   . . . . . if some lapidary had the stone,
        more would not buy it than I can demand.
        'Tis as well set, I think, as ere ye saw.
KING.   'Tis set, indeed upon the fairest hand
        that e'er I saw.
JANE.   You are disposed to jest. But for value
        his maiestie might wear it.
KING.   Might he, ifaith?
JANE.   Sir, 'tis the ring I mean.
KING.   I meant the hand.[24]

Jane says that the king looks like a chapman, as her
unloving husband was. The king reveals himself to
Jane, and offers his love, but she does not yield to
him then.[25]

The irony and dramatic foreshadowing is further
intensified by the entrance of Shore himself. This keen
salesman interprets their subdued conversation into a
haggling over the price of some article, and thinks that
he can persuade the king to buy more easily than his
wife can. The king, continuing, says:

        Youle not be offered fairlier I beleeve.
JANE.   Indeed, you offer like a gentleman;
        But yet the jewell will not so be left.
SHORE.   Sir, if you bid not too much under-foot,
        I'll drive the bargain twixt you and my wife.

[24] Pages 64 and 65.   [25] Page 66.

KING.   *(aside)* Alas, good Shore, myself dare answer No.
        Nothing can make thee such a jewell foregoe.
        She saith you shall be too much loser by it.
SHORE. See in the row, then, if you can speede
        better.

Matthew Shore is discontented on seeing that it is the king, and becomes suspicious of his motive.

> Keep we our treasure secret, yet so fond
> As set so rich a beauty as this is
> In the wide view of every gazer's eye?[26]

Jane ponders, but eventually accepts the king's proposal, and becomes his paramour. She is partly persuaded by Mistress Blague, a neighbor, who pictures vividly to Jane the sovereignty and renown that she will have in court.

From several ballads on the subject of Jane Shore one that may be briefly considered is *The Woeful Lamentation of Jane Shore, a goldsmith's Wife in London, sometime King Edward the Fourths Concubine in two parts.*[27] Tragic, moral, romantic, poetic (sung to the tune of *Live with me*), it has realism as to the goldsmith's craft, and illustrates powerfully the aspiration of a craftswoman to nobility.

Matthew Shore, the goldsmith, describes Jane's circumstances as his wife, before she had committed adultery with the king:

> No London Dame, nor merchant's Wife,
> Did lead so sweet and pleasant life.

[26] Page 68.
[27] Phillips' *Old Ballads*, vol. 1, p. 145. Other ballads dealing with her are Deloney's *Lamentation of Shore's Wife* and a burlesque called *King Edward and Jane Shore.*

> Thou hadst both gold and silver store,

He describes how in Turkey he

> set thy Picture there in gold,
> For Kings and Princes to behold.[25]

Thus it was that Jane's parents had married her while she was young to one of the richest representatives of a wealthy and honorable craft. But is Jane satisfied? She has wealth and dignity, but no love for her husband. Exhibited by him in his shop to attract customers, her great beauty naturally attracts many highborn admirers.

> If Rosamond that was so fair,
> Had cause her sorrows to declare;
> Then let Jane Shore with sorrow sing,
> That was beloved of a King.
> Then wanton wives in time amend,
> For Love and Beauty will have end.[29]

> In Maiden years my Beauty bright
> Was loved dear by Lord and Knight,
> But yet the Love that they required,
> It was not as my Friends desir'd.
> . . . .

> To Matthew Shore I was a Wife,
> Till Lust brought Ruin to my life,
> And then my life I lewdly spent,
> Which makes my Soul for to lament.

> In Lombard street I once did dwell,
> As London yet can witness well,
> Where many gallants did behold

[25] These quotations are from Part 2 of the ballad, Roxburghe Ballads, vol. 2, p. 115.
[29] The last two lines of this stanza form the refrain.

My Beauty in a Shop of gold.[10]
. . . .
At last my name in Court did ring
Into the Ears of England's King,
Who came and lik'd, and love requir'd,
But I made coy what he desir'd:

Yet mistress Blague, a Neighbour near,
Whose Friendship I esteemed dear,
Did say, *It is a gallant thing*
To be beloved of a King.[11]
. . . .

So it is that Jane Shore yields to the temptation
of riches and fame. Advanced to high power by the
king, she is philanthropic and honored. After King
Edward IV dies, his successor, Richard III, forces Jane
to do public penance as a whore.

Massinger's *City Madam*, 1632, also presents trouble
brought to bear upon city women and apprentices who
are dissatisfied with their social station. The wife and
daughters, Anne and Mary, of Sir John Frugal, a
prosperous merchant, have "hopes above their birth"
of becoming countesses. Their dress is in harmony
with these anticipations; they wear, moreover, mirrors
at their girdles. Superstitious as many such uncultured
people are, they have a star-gazer study their fortunes
for them. These women show an advance over the
aspirations even of Gertrude in *Eastward Hoe*. She
desired to have a coach, to marry a knight, and thus

[10] Note the frequency with which gold is mentioned. This
applies also to Part 2.
[11] Heywood in *Edward IV*, Part 1, 1874 ed., vol. 1, p. 75,
similarly depicts the fascination that court life has for Jane
Shore and for people of her class. These are the words of
mistress Blague:
"Now mistress Shore, bethink ye what to do,
Such suitors come not every day to woo."

be called "lady." These daughters in *The City Madam* even go so far as to specify the kind of coach, the kind of cooks, French and Italian, and they not only wish to be called "lady," but also to have complete sovereignty over their future husbands. Anne wants coaches, each drawn by four Flanders mares.[32] Mary desires even more: she wants the more fashionable country sports, large manors, countless cattle, and to have such complete power over her husband that she will be spoken of as Lady Plenty, and her husband never mentioned.

These proud women, however, are soon humbled, for Luke, the brother of Sir John Frugal, gains control over John's goods and forces the women to wear old clothes and take subordinate positions as a penalty for their affectations.

Several of Shirley's plays have fashionable women who are more successful than Gertrude in *Eastward Hoe* is in disguising their low descent: they do not utter words unconsciously that reveal their former associations with the city trades.

Shirley's *Hyde Park*, 1632, is a fair illustration. Mistress Bonavent, who is supposed to be the widow of a merchant, wishes to marry again.[33] She does not need to desire some of these attributes of wealth as the women previously mentioned do; she already has them, but is discontented. She has command, attendants, jewels, a coach, a livery, a monkey, a squirrel, and a

---

[32] Flanders mares are very expensive and fashionable animals. In Glapthorne's *Wit in a Constable*, 1639, Clare, the niece of an alderman, despises craftsmen, their dress, manners, etc., and she says that she will marry only one who can give her a coach and four horses.

[33] Her husband is in reality still alive.

tailor of her own. Her fashionable and idle life is very different from the industry of the wives depicted in Deloney's fiction.

We shall now say something about the development of the apprentice in the hands of authors, as this, like the craftsman's wife, is a stock figure in the literature. In the Middle Ages the rigid system of apprenticeship doubtless held many youths in check that would otherwise have been led astray. But with the Renaissance, emphasis on institutions was superseded by individualism: the apprentice came to realize his importance as a civic and even as a national figure, hence the emphasis laid on the warlike and patriotic apprentice in all forms of the literature of the period from 1590-1600 especially.[34]

Interest in battles, armies, processions, and shows, fostered by the writings of Deloney, Heywood, and Rowley, who appeal to apprentices, leads gradually to the apprentices' indolence and slackness in work, to their frequenting of theaters, taverns, and gambling houses.

The best general description of the apprentices of shopkeepers and craftsmen, and of their chores and amusements is by a late writer, Shirley, in his *Honoria and Mammon*, 1639. Squanderbag compares the life of a soldier to that of an apprentice:

> Is not this better than a tedious 'prenticeship,
> Bound by indentures to a shop and drudgery,
> Watching the rats and customers by owl-light?
> Tied to perpetual language of, What lack ye?

[34] This theme continues almost until the closing of the theaters in scattered works; e. g., Rawlins' *Rebellion*, 1639, a rough copy of Rowley's *Shoomaker a Gentleman*, 1609.

Which you pronounce, as ye had been taught, like starlings:
If any gudgeon bite, to damn your souls
For less than sixpence in the pound? Oh base!
Your glittering shoes, long graces, and short meals,
Expecting but the comfortable hour
Of eight o'clock, and the hot pippin-pies,
To wake your mouth up? All the day not suffered
To air yourselves, unless your minikin mistress
Command you to attend her to a christ'ning,
To bring home plums......................
You have some festivals, I confess, but when
They happen, you run wild to the next village,
Conspire a knot, and club your groats a-piece
For cream and prunes, not daring to be drunk;
Nothing of honour done. Now you are gentlemen,
And in capacity to be all commanders,
If you dare fight.[35]

We have riotous and extravagant apprentices in several plays, *Eastward Hoe*, 1605, being a good illustration. Quicksilver, the goldsmith's apprentice of this play, wears gay clothes and a sword, visits theaters and quotes freely from the more spectacular and popular plays of the period. He is dishonest, having learned much trickery in the goldsmith's craft, trickery which he can easily employ anywhere. He also understands well the nature of others, and deceives Gertrude, his master's daughter, by working on her childish desire for fine clothes and a coach. In the same play there is an industrious fellow-apprentice of Quicksilver called Golding, who by perseverance and honesty gradually wins the good will of his master and becomes an alderman's deputy and magistrate.

Just as the ballad on Jane Shore serves as a warning to the craftsman's wife who is discontented with her

[35] Act 5, sc. 1.

station in life, so also certain ballads are directed against the wayward apprentice. *An excellent Ballad of George Barnwell*[36] describes a thievish, lustful, and murderous apprentice. It has a moral and tragic note, as has also George Lillo's tragedy, *George Barnwell, or the London Merchant,* 1731. This ballad was often used as a warning to apprentices. Like the ballad on Jane Shore, the present one is forcible and dramatic partly because of its being told in the first person. George, the apprentice, tells how he was tempted by a harlot to steal his master's money and run away. Fascinated by her, he is led to murder his master and rich uncle for their money. After the money is all spent, the harlot deserts him. Both culprits are caught and sentenced to execution.

The next ballad to be considered has more realistic touches as to the craft of the apprentice; i. e., that of a goldsmith. It is called *A Ballad,* and dated 1576, in the Stationer's Company.[37] George Mannington disobeys the statutes against gorgeous attire of apprentices. After he is arrested for his misdeeds, he sings as follows:

> I had a master good and kinde,
> That would have wrought me to his minde.
> . . . .
> False mettall of good manners I
> Did daily coyne unlawfully.
> . . . .
> Now cried I, Touch-stone,[38] touch me still,

[36] Percy Socy. Pub., vol. 1, p. 35. It is in two parts.
[37] Percy Socy. Pub., vol. 1, p. 51.
[38] Touch-stone is his master. A touchstone is also a stone used by goldsmiths to test the purity of gold and silver. Note the number of technical expressions.

And make me current by thy skill.

. . . .

Farewell, Cheapside, farewell, sweet trade
Of goldsmiths all, that never shall fade,
Farewell, dear fellow prentices all,
And be you warned by my fall.
Shun usurer's bonds etc.[39]

Cooke's *Greenes tu Quoque*, 1614,[40] and Mayne's *City
Match*, 1639, depict extravagant and riotous apprentices. In the former, Spendall, a mercer's apprentice,
is suddenly made master of the shop, on his master's
being knighted. Spendall is carried away by his un-
expected advance, and has an expectation that he will
some day become Lord Mayor:

A Lord? by this light, I do not think but to be Lord Mayor
of London before I die, and have three pageants carried before
me, besides a ship and an unicorn. Prentices may pray for that
time; for, whenever it happens, I will make another Shrove
Tuesday for them.[41]

He becomes extravagant, squandering his money on
dice games, and is finally arrested for his extravagance.
In *The City Match*, Plotwell, a grocer's apprentice, is
lured from his trade by Templars to see an extravagant
lady. He is easily led to despise his trade on being
called "base mechanic,"[42] and becomes riotous. In both

[39] This alludes to the custom of goldsmiths, as well as of
several richer types of craftsmen, of lending out money on
usury.

These verses are appropriately read by Quicksilver, the goldsmith's riotous apprentice in *Eastward Hoe*, as he is in prison
for debt and misdeeds.

[40] The date of writing is uncertain. It is in Dodsley's *Old
English Plays*, vol. 7.

[41] Page 19.

[42] Act 1, sc. 4.

of these plays a keen interest is shown by craftsmen in pageants and spectacles.

Massinger's *City Madam*, 1632, shows some variation in the delineation of apprentices from that in *Eastward Hoe*. As in the two preceding plays, the two apprentices, Goldwire and Tradewell, are bound, not to a mean shopkeeper, but to a great speculating merchant, Sir John Frugal. They are, moreover, sons of gentlemen, a fact which increases their pride. They are, therefore, not only interested in fine clothes, but also in the larger aspects of nobility, such as the possession of estates. In talking of Frugal's many ventures, they mention his buying of manors. Luke Frugal, the merchant's brother, appealing to the respectable caste of the apprentices, and holding out to them the joy of going in a coach to Brentford, of having attendants, and of wearing the attire of gallants, tempts them to become rich by stealing from their master's wealth of which they are stewards:

> Are you Gentlemen born, yet have no gallant Tincture
> Of Gentry in you? you are no mechanicks,
> Nor serve some needy Shop-keeper, who surveys
> His Every-day-takings.[43]

After these apprentices have embezzled from their master, Luke, who is a great hypocrite, has them arrested on a charge of conspiracy against his brother. To their complaining fathers he says that masters never prospered since gentlemen's sons became apprentices, for they are too frequently at tennis courts and ordinaries.[44]

[43] Act 2, sc. 1.
[44] Act 5, sc. 1. As does Massinger's *New Way to Pay Old Debts*, this play shows the enmity between the noble born and the self-made man.

Writers of some importance in this treatment of low born city people who have attained social eminence are James Shirley and Richard Brome, a follower of Jonson. In their treatment of such people who are or have been artisans or are at least relatives of artisans, they frequently represent them as having successfully cast off their crude manners of the city artisans. They are thus representing artisans who seem very dissimilar to those represented by Deloney, Dekker, Heywood, or Rowley.

Brome's *New Academy,* 1658, shows more clearly than any play thus far considered the advance of the apprentices over their dependent positions as described in earlier works, and illustrates well the intermarrying between the highborn and the low born.

Cash, an apprentice to a successful merchant, Matchill, is frequently at feasts and revels, and dresses in silver lace and satin. In this finery he appears at dances with gallants, some of whom are in debt to his own master. Cash is an excellent picture of an apprentice, but one of a special kind, entirely unlike the unsophisticated ones of earlier writers such as Deloney and Dekker. Strigood differentiates him from the low type of apprentice who goes with his sweetheart to Islington or Hogsden for prunes, cream, and ale.

> As for his bravery
> 'Tis no new thing with him, I know him of old.
> This sute's his worst of foure.
> And he's one
> Of the foure famous Prentices o' th' time.
> None of the Cream and Cake-boys, nor of those,
> That gall their hands with....., or their cat-sticks,

For white-pots, pudding-pies, stew'd prunes, and Tansies.
To feast their Titts at Islington or Hogsden.
But haunts the famous Ordinaries o' th' time,
Where the best chear, best game, best company are frequent.
Lords call him Cousin at the Bowling Green;
And the great Tennis-Court.[45]

Certain it is that Cash does not reveal by his talk or actions that he is an apprentice. Cash is, moreover, a man of the world, with a ready action by which to extricate himself when he is involved in any suspicion of a scandal.

After long attempts to imitate fashionable society, it seems that the apprentices and city women as depicted by Shirley and Brome have succeeded in losing their former crudeness.

Much has already been said, especially in connection with the Lord Mayor Show, about the admiration that artisans had for dramatic and pageantic spectacles. They took a keen interest in the display of fine clothing, processions, or emotions. A well known illustration of this is in Shakespeare's *Midsummer Night's Dream*, 1594-5. Six craftsmen : Quince, a carpenter; Snug, a joiner; Bottom, a weaver; Flute, a bellows-mender; Snout, a tinker; and Starveling, a tailor, present an interlude on the wedding night of Duke Theseus of Athens. Their childish clumsiness and love of imitation are well represented. The juxtaposition of realism and pseudo-romanticism which lacks the necessary imagination on the part of the artisans is one source of the humor. Bottom wants to be Pyramus, Thisbe, and the lion, as he likes to roar. Each actor clumsily ex-

---

[45] Act 3, sc. 2. There are references here to the servile task that apprentices of the meaner trades were obliged to do, if they wished spending money.

plains his part, having little knowledge of stage conventions, and blunders on certain words; e. g., Pyramus calls "Ninus' tomb" "Ninny's tomb."[46]

In several of Jonson's plays are criticisms of the clumsy theatrical performances of amateurs. In his *Tale of a Tub*, 1633, To-Pan, a tinker, Medlay, a cooper, and Clay, a tile-maker, take part in a play. Medlay, the original and self-centered cooper who designs the masque, claims to have upon his rule the just proportions of a knight or squire.[47] In Jonson's *Bartholomew Fair*, 1614, there is a puppet show[48] representing the story of Hero and Leander. Leander is a dyer's son in Puddle-Wharf. The story of Damon and Pythias is confused with this, and the ghost of Dionysius appears on the stage. Humor is furnished by the futile attempts of Busy, the Puritan baker, to break up the show.

A favorite subject of craftsmen for presentation on the stage is knight-errantry and patriotism, especially when the heroes of such romances are from the craftsmen's own ranks. Heywood's *Four Prentices of London*, 1600 c., is a good illustration of this type, a type which meets with ridicule in the hands of Beaumont and Fletcher and Jonson.

The best satire on craftsmen's thirsting for military renown is Beaumont and Fletcher's *Knight of the Burning Pestle*, 1611. A citizen is going to have something represented on the stage in honor of his grocer's trade. At his wife's suggestion, who also takes keen interest in it, he will have a hero kill a lion with a pestle. Ralph, his apprentice, is given the chief part,

---

[46] Act 5, sc. 1.   [47] Act 4, sc. 2.
                  [48] Act 5, sc. 3.

and because of his grocer's trade he calls himself the
"Knight of the Burning Pestle." One apprentice is his
dwarf; another is his squire. He constantly imitates
the language of chivalry; e. g., that of *Palmerin,* an
old chivalric romance, and quotes Hotspur's speech
about honor in *Henry IV,* Part 1.[49] Although Ralph
has pledged himself to defend Mistress Merrythought,
who is in trouble, he runs away as soon as his pestle
has been seized. He goes to fight against a giant,
Barbarossa,[50] who turns out to be only a barber. Ralph
knocks him down, and frees his prisoners, who have
been tortured in various ways by the barber's quack
surgery. One has had stinging powder applied to cure
the itch; another has had the gristle of his nose cut
off; others are kept in a hot tub as a cure for syphilis.
Ralph falls in love with Susan, a cobbler's maid, who
has inspired him to do these deeds of arms. His master
is so pleased with his performances that he will make
him next year the captain of the Lord Mayor's barge.

In Shirley's interlude, *A Contention for Honor and
Riches,* 1633, and in his morality, *Honoria and Mammon,* 1659, are satirical thrusts at the Lord Mayor's
Show. In the former,[51] Clod, a country fellow, ridicules
civic officers, shop-keepers, and Lord Mayor Shows
with ships swimming upon men's shoulders.

Two ballads among others which satirize the Lord
Mayor's Show are *Oh London is a fine Town*[52] and

[49] Other instances of the burlesque on tales of chivalry are in
the character of Puntarvolo in *Every Man Out of his Humor*
and in Petronel in *Eastward Hoe.*

[50] Act 3, sc. 4.

[51] Scene 1.

[52] D'Urfey's *Pills to Purge Melancholy,* vol. 4, p. 40.

Upon my Lord Maior's Day, being put off by reason of the Plague.[53] In the latter the mayor is "forbad to goe a feasting in his scarlet gown."

> Nor shall they hear the players tall,
> Who mounted on some mighty whale,
> Swim with him through Cheapside.

Craftsmen welcome any occasion for displaying spectacular things, and are most pleased by the presentation of something exciting. In Tatham's play, *The Rump*, 1660, apprentices externalize their dissatisfaction with the Rump Parliament by burning rumps of mutton in public. In the Fishmongers' Lord Mayor Shows, Sir William Walworth, former Mayor and fishmonger, frequently appears, bearing the head of the rebel, Wat Tyler, whom he had slain. In Mark Antony's speech to the mob in *Julius Caesar*, he works upon the excitability of those present, increasing their pity by showing the rent mantle of Caesar and then Caesar's own bloody corpse, stabbed in several places.

Indeed, Shakespeare, who will be considered more fully later, is as excellent as any other writer in his delineation of craftsmen in crowds, and their love of sights. Although the craftsmen in literature like most of all to see represented on the stage military exploits of their own members, they also glorify a military hero apart from their ranks if he offers a sufficiently spectacular career. Thus, in *Julius Caesar*, 1599, the interest of the fickle mob (a fair part of which is composed of artisans) is centered on three military heroes successively, Pompey, Caesar, and Brutus, in honor of whom they wish to give pageants and spec-

---

[53] Percy Socy., vol. 1, p. 28.

tacles.[54] In *Coriolanus,* 1609, it is Coriolanus' stubborn
and tactless refusal to cater to the craftsmen's extreme
love of a spectacle and dramatic speech, that brings
about the tragedy. In *Antony and Cleopatra,* 1607-8,
Cleopatra fears that the base "mechanic slaves" will
stage her tragic fall, and perhaps turn it into a vulgar
comedy.[55]

> Thou, an Egyptian puppet, shalt be shown
> In Rome, as well as I: mechanic slaves,
> With greasy aprons, rules, and hammers, shall
> Uplift us to the view; in their thick breaths,
> Rank of gross diet, shall we be enclouded,
> and forced to drink their vapour.
>
> .... saucy lictors
> Will catch at us, like strumpets; and scald rhymers
> Ballad us out o' tune: the quick comedians
> Extemporally will stage us, and present
> Our Alexandrian revels; Antony
> Shall be brought drunken forth, and I shall see
> Some squeaking Cleopatra boy my greatness
> I' the posture of a whore.[56]

In a previous chapter much has been said about
works that praise craftsmen in battle. There are,
however, reactions in the period of James I and
Charles I to this adulation of craftsmen in battle. Two
works that present citizens in general as desiring a
disreputable peace rather than a settling of the trouble
by fighting are Cartwright's *The Siege,* acted before

[54] In the three Roman plays, the mob is said to be composed
largely of Roman artisans, but they have the traits of English
ones.

[55] Act 5, sc. 2. Cleopatra says these words to Iras.

[56] Boy actors took the roles of women in Pre-Restoration
drama.

1643,[57] and Shakespeare's *King John*, 1593. Several
miscellaneous works represent craftsmen as ridicu-
lous in their attempts at fighting. Thus, in Mayne's
Amorous War, 1648, the Bithynian craftsmen, in fighting against Thrace, arm themselves with appropriate
weapons: butchers with cleavers, tailors with yards
and bodkins, and shoemakers with awls.[58] They are
clumsy and unorganized when it comes to fighting. In
Beaumont and Fletcher's *Philaster*, the captain exhorts
the citizens to leave their base crafts and to fight
nobly; i. e., even though they are craftsmen.[59] In *The
Famous Victories of Henry V* and in Rowley's *Shoomaker a Gentleman*[60] the cobbler is a cowardly type
of fighter. *A Larum for London*, printed in 1602, and
*The Famous History of the Life and Death of Captain
Thomas Stukeley*, printed in 1605,[61] bring out the fact
that trained soldiers are more successful fighters than
citizens or craftsmen. In *A Larum for London*,[62] the
citizens with poor success try to beat back the opposing
Spaniards.

> We are undone for want of discipline.[63]

Craftsmen are frequently represented as the leaders

[57] Printed for H. Moseley, 1651.

[58] Act 1, sc. 2.

[59] Act 5, sc. 1.

[60] This play has been considered carefully in the preceding
chapter. The prince, Crispianus, who is for a time apprentice
to a shoemaker, fights nobly; Barnaby, the journeyman, on the
other hand, is a cowardly type of soldier.

[61] R. Simpson's *School of Shakespeare*, vol. 1. Stukeley was
a rich clothier's son, according to a ballad on him. According
to Deloney's *Gentle Craft*, Part 2, Stukeley is several times
defeated by Peachy, a shoemaker.

[62] Malone Society Reprints, 1913.

[63] Line 630.

or members of popular uprisings. Hardly any of these
works are flattering to craftsmen, for they are represented here as lacking in bravery, organization, and
decision. In *The Life and Death of Jack Straw*, 1593,[64]
the artisan-soldiers are alluded to thus:

> ....they
> Be none but tilers, thatchers, millers, and such like,
> That in their lives did never come in field.[65]

In *Woodstock*[66] a butcher shows great discontent with
the existing government; and in Shirley's *Arcadia*,
1640, Thumb, a miller, puts himself at the head of
the rebels, but is lacking when it comes to actual
fighting.

A play of this type that delineates craftsmen with
realism is Ford's *Perkin Warbeck*, printed in 1634.
*The First Part of the Contention of the two famous
Houses of Yorke and Lancaster*, 1590; and Shakes-
peare's *Henry VI*, Part 2, 1590-2, which follows the
Contention in the parts that deal with the artisan-rebel,
Jack Cade, are other instances.

The first of these plays represents Perkin as sup-
ported in his uprising by Heron, a bankrupt mercer;
John a Water, the mayor of Cork; Skelton, a tailor;
and Astley, a scrivener. Heron and Skelton are individualized well. Heron had aspired to be "a viscount
at least," even when he traded but in remnants.[67]
Skelton's references to terms from his own trade for
metaphors is interesting.

[64] Dodsley's *Old English Plays*, vol. 5.
[65] Act 1.
[66] *Jahrbuch der Deutschen Shakespeare Gesellschaft*, 1899.
[67] Act 2, sc. 3, p. 153, Dyce edition.

..... he that threads his needle with the sharp eyes of industry shall in time go through-stitch with the new suit of preferment.[68]

Skelton also speaks of the pressing-iron of reproach.

These artisans are far from brave: when captured, they quail before King Henry VII, in strong contrast to Warbeck, who conducts himself throughout the play with fearless and dignified demeanor.

There is more of the element of satire in *The First Part of the Contention etc.* and in Shakespeare's *Henry VI*, Part 2. In the *Contention*[69] are several realistic touches on craft. An illustration apart from the Jack Cade rebellion is the quarrel between an armorer and his apprentice, a story which is paralleled in Shakespeare's play.[70]

Several apprentices speak of Cade, the leader of the rebels, as follows:

GEORGE.   Jack Cade the Diar[71] of Ashford here,
          He means to turne this land, and set a new nap on it.
NICK.   I marry he had need so, for 'tis growne threedbare...
GEORGE.   I warrant thee, thou shalt never see a Lord weare a
          leather aperne nowadaies.
NICK.   But sirrha, who comes more beside Jacke Cade?
GEORGE.   Why theres Dicke the Butcher, and Robin the Sadler,
          and Will etc., and we must all be Lords or squires, as
          soone as Jacke Cade is King.[72]

Cade boasts about his bravery, asserts that his father was a Mortemer, and calls himself Lord Mortemer. The artisans nearby whisper to one another that Cade's

---

[68] Act 2, sc. 3, p. 154.
[69] Facsimile Text.
[70] Act 1, sc. 3.
[71] "Diar;" i. e., dyer.
[72] In *Henry VI* also the artisans are well portrayed.

father was a bricklayer, and that his mother was the daughter of a peddler.

Trying to gain the support of a rabble composed partly of artisans, Cade appeals to them in various ways; e. g., he endows a butcher with greater trade privileges than he has had hitherto, promises them all plenty of beer, and knights himself and them. Cruel and destructive, he has a clerk hanged because he can write (reading or writing being accomplishments hateful to Cade) ; and has London Bridge burned. Like Leyden, the tailor who leads the Munster rebels,[73] Cade is socialistic and defends stealing. According to him, wives are common property. Another point of resemblance between Cade's situation and Leyden's is that Cade nearly starves, and lives on herbs.

This rebel has no personality or leadership. The fragments of his army, like himself, lack organizing power, and vacillate between Cade and his more victorious opponent, Clifford. Cade is finally killed by one of his own group, Eyden, who is desirous of obtaining knighthood and the thousand crowns offered for Cade's head.

Something has already been seen in these previously mentioned works about the inconsistency of mobs, composed to an extent of artisans. *Sir Thomas More*, 1590, contains a good picture of a mob, the hatred of which is directed especially against foreign merchants and artisans who displace English craftsmen.[74] There is a vivid presentation of apprentices, armed with clubs,[75] who burn the houses of foreigners and release

[73] This is well satirized in Rowland's *Hells Broke Loose*.
[74] Shakespeare Socy., vol. 3; Dyce edition, 1844. The play borrows something from Hall's *Chronicle*, fol. 59 (b), ed. 1548.
[75] Page 17.

the prisoners. In their wild clamor about their griev-
ances, they lack general and wholehearted nationality,
are greatly swayed by personal prejudices and private
desires. An instance is in the desire of Doll, the wife
of a carpenter, to hear Sir Thomas More speak:

> ..... a made my brother Arthur Watchins Seriant
> Safes yeoman: lets heare Shreeve More.[76]

Like the members of the mob in *Julius Caesar*, these
are appeased by More's eloquent and tactful speech,
which upholds the divine right of kings, condemns
rebellion, and appeals to the emotion rather than to
the reason of the listeners.

A ballad which, like the play just described, deals
with the hatred of English toward foreign merchants
or artisans is *The Story of Ill May-Day in the time
of King Henry VIII.*[77] It tells of the uprising of English
artisans on May-eve, 1517, against foreigners who
monopolized their trade. The rebels free those who
have been imprisoned for hostility to foreigners.

In the treatment of artisans as members of a mob,
rather than as individuals, Shakespeare is supreme.
Although he does not deny that the citizen or artisan
is of some importance in the state (as is shown by
the fact that Bolingbroke, afterwards King Henry IV,
Gloster, and Mark Antony seek the support of the
citizens or mayor), he shows (following the dramatic
tradition of his time) little admiration or sympathy
for the laboring man *en masse*. He usually emphasizes
the meaner qualities of artificers: susceptibility to
flattery, fickleness, inconsistency, avarice, and craving

---

[76] **Page 26,** line 17.
[77] **Evans'** *Old Ballads*, vol. 3, p. 15.

for social recognition by great ones. Hence, in *Romeo and Juliet*, 1594-5,[78] citizens with clubs join in the fray between the servants of the house of Montague and the house of Capulet. It is mainly because these citizens like to get into a quarrel; some of them show no preference for either house. In *King Henry VIII*, likewise, 1612, the noisiness of apprentices and their readiness to decide quarrels by the use of clubs and stones are emphasized.[79] The porter comments on the fact that these are the noisy youths so boisterous in playhouses.

More interesting for our study is Shakespeare's treatment of the artisan as related to nobility or royalty. Much has been already said about the desire of artisans for recognition by knights or kings. The Lord Mayor's Show, as beforesaid, frequently illustrates this; e. g., in the Merchant-Taylors' Show, great pride is manifested in the fact that many kings and nobles were free of that company. The presentation by artisans of plays and pageants on royal occasions is brought out in Shakespeare's *Midsummer Night's Dream* and *Henry VIII*[80] respectively. In the latter play, the citizens are said to take great interest in the coronation ceremony of Queen Anne, and to prepare pageants for the occasion.

Attention will be given to several plays of Shakespeare in which demagogues obtain popularity through appealing by promises, courtesy, flattery, etc., to mobs consisting in large measure of craftsmen.

We shall first consider *Richard II*, 1595. Bolingbroke, the cousin of Richard II, whom the king has banished, understands well the various subtle arts by which he

[78] Act 1, sc. 1.   [79] Act. 5, sc. 3.
                   [80] Act 4, sc. 1.

may obtain the friendship of the commons. Taking
advantage of the king's unpopularity, partly due to the
heavy taxation and social unrest of the period, Bolingbroke represents himself as the special friend of the
common people: the trading and working classes. He
therefore misses no opportunity of smirking at them
and showing them various courtesies. The king, after
banishing Bolingbroke, describes him as follows:

> Ourself and Bushy, Bagot here and Green
> Observed his courtship to the common people;
> How he did seem to dive into their hearts
> With humble and familiar courtesy,
> What reverence he did throw away on slaves,
> Wooing poor craftsmen with the craft of smiles
> And patient underbearing of his fortune,
> As 'twere to banish their affects with him.
> Off goes his bonnet to an oyster-wench;
> A brace of draymen bid God speed him well
> And had the tribute of his supple knee,
> With 'Thanks, my countrymen, my loving friends;'
> As were our England in reversion his,
> And he our subjects' next degree in hope.[81]

The most excellent pictures of mobs consisting largely
of artisans are in *Julius Caesar*, 1599, and *Coriolanus*,
1609.

In *Julius Caesar* many aspects of the working people's nature are brought out. Though these are called
Roman citizens and artificers, they answer well for a
delineation of English ones. The love of the artisans
for holidays and spectacles is brought out in the first

---

[81] Act 1, sc. 4, lines 23-36.

A parallel may be noted in this outcast's tactful behavior to
that of the dethroned King Edward IV, as described in Bulwer-
Lytton's *Last of the Barons*. Both of these statesmen appeal
strongly to the commercial classes.

scene. In this feast of Lupercal various craftsmen are presented; the leader, a shoemaker, one from the popular guild of the late 16th century, is especially witty. He puns on certain words peculiar to his craft: "mend," "sole," and "awl." These artisans are assembled to celebrate Caesar's triumph. Their fickleness and inconsistency are well described by Marullus, the tribune. The latter reminds them that they had formerly made as much ceremony and display over Pompey, Caesar's enemy, when Pompey passed in triumphal chariot through the Roman streets. Their fickleness and love of pomp may also be seen in their wishing later to crown and celebrate Brutus, and last of all, making even Antony a popular hero.[82] In Casca's story of the offering of the crown to Caesar[83] the undesirable qualities of craftsmen are stressed: they have "chopped hands," "sweaty night-caps," and "stinking breath."

After the assassination of Caesar, the artisans exhibit their tendency to settle all things by violence, by a club law, as it were.[84] Brutus appeals to their nobler sentiments by suggesting that they are patriotic freemen and not base bondmen, he satisfies them, even though he gives no sound explanation as to his reason for killing Caesar. They are quieted temporarily with the feeling that Caesar was killed because he was ambitious, "ambitious" being a word which, as it

[82] That some of these craftsmen appear also at Antony's speech seems evident from the fact that he refers to their witnessing the offer of the crown to Caesar on the Lupercal.

[83] Act 1, sc. 2.
It must be borne in mind, however, that Casca is a sour person, tending to belittle whatever he describes.

[84] The stage directions do not mention clubs. In Robert Mantell's presentation of the play, however, these citizens are armed with clubs, like unruly apprentices.

appears later, they do not understand, but vaguely
suppose has something to do with tyranny. In their
tendency to furnish a popular hero for any occasion,
they desire to bring Brutus home with triumph, to give
him a statue with his ancestors, and (which further
confirms the fact that they do not understand the
reason for the assassination) to crown Brutus, the
assassin of the very Caesar whom they had previously
wished to celebrate.

Now that Brutus has left them with a vague idea
of Caesar's "ambition," it remains for Antony to dis-
lodge that attribute of Caesar from their minds. He
pretends, therefore, in a flattering way, to appeal to
their reason; but he actually appeals to their emotion,
avarice, admiration for large estates and for world
power.

> He hath brought many captives home to Rome,
> Whose ransom did the general coffers fill.

What could appeal more forcibly to an excitable crowd
whose tendency is to glorify military heroes? What
could appeal more to the hearers' avarice than the same
sentence?

> When that the poor have cried, Caesar hath wept,
> Ambition should be made of sterner stuff.

What could appeal more to their sympathy than this
gentler attribute of the great conqueror, whose ten-
derness seems to have leaned to just such people as
themselves? To the uncultured artisans so excited by
dramatic and spectacular scenes, what could appeal
more than Antony's presentation of Caesar's mantle
and body and his vivid characterization of each of

the conspirators cruelly butchering the great national demigod?

The above words illustrate how emotional these commons are: Antony's appeal is not to reason or judgment. Of the three reasons why Caesar was not "ambitious:" 1, that he enriched the country as a whole; 2, that he wept for the poor; 3, that he thrice refused a crown, only the last has any connection with ambition. Moreover, if we take Casca's words as to Caesar's unwillingness to refuse the crown, it is not even an indication, far less a proof, that Caesar was not ambitious.

In *Coriolanus,* stubborn insistence of craftsmen on form and timeworn ceremonies, and Coriolanus's refusal to comply are large determining factors in the tragedy. The mutinous citizens represent English craftsmen.[85] The hungry citizens, armed with clubs, threaten the government if they are not fed immediately. The tactful Menenius quiets them by his fable which represents them as having a definite place in the government. Marcius (later Coriolanus) casts several aspersions on them, calling them "gnawing rats,"[86] describes their fickleness, and their preference for a man's bows and flattery rather than his heart. Even to gain the consulship, he does not intend to show the commons the many wounds which he has received

---

[85] That the mob is composed in large part of craftsmen is attested to in Coriolanus' words to his mother:
> "Do not bid me
> Dismiss my soldiers, or capitulate
> Again with Rome's mechanics."
> Act 5, sc. 3.

[86] Cf. Shirley's *Doubtful Heir* in which a captain expresses a similar attitude toward craftsmen. Act 1.

in battle.[87] Though craftsmen seem to make a fair
proportion of the fighting body, Coriolanus is probably
correct in saying that they are base born cowards,[88]
having often deserted in battle. Though he exaggerates
frequently, he would not be apt to tell an absolute lie.

Coriolanus is finally persuaded to conform to the
custom of the commons by showing his wounds and
saying something to them, a form of procedure which
he does contemptuously. He is then elected consul. The
tribunes, however, call the attention of the citizens to
the scornful way in which Coriolanus had shown his
wounds, and his sarcastic manner of address.[89] The
artisans[90] are so exasperated that they withdraw their
former election of him as consul, and effect his banish-
ment from the city.

When the citizens hear that a Volscian invasion,
partly led by Coriolanus, is threatened, some assert
that they did not want to banish him.

These two Roman plays of Shakespeare picture excellently well the inability of uncultured artisans (or
uncultured persons of any kind) to act as statesmen
or electors of statesmen. Fickle, tending to extol a
hero at one moment, and to destroy him at the next;
unreliable, inclined to worship rank rather than prin-
ciple, the craftsmen in these plays are well pictured as

[87] Act 2, sc. 1.
[88] Act 2, sc. 3.
[89] Act 2, sc. 3.
[90] That artisans have a large part in this seems evident
from Menenius' ironic words to the tribunes regarding their
unstatesmanlike behavior:
"You have made fair hands,
You and your crafts! You have crafted fair!"
Act 4, sc. 6, lines 115-116.

failures in their attempts to interfere with the government.[91]
Several miscellaneous works describe artisans as leaders or members of popular uprisings. In verse there is Daniel's treatment of the Jack Cade rebellion in his *Civil Wars*.[92] In prose there are Lodge's *Life and Death of William Longbeard*, and Rowlands' *Runnagates Race* (in his *Martin Markall*). The following satirical prose works of Taylor combine an interest in communism with fanatic religious zeal: *The Whole Life and Progresse of Henry Walker the Iron-monger, Jack a Lent, A Tale in a Tub*, and *A Full and compleat Answer Against the Writer of a Tale in a Tub*.

The Munster uprising is treated in the prose work, *Mock-Majesty: or, The Siege of Munster*, and Leyden is described in Nash's *Unfortunate Traveller*; but the best satirical treatment is given in Rowlands' poem, *Hells Broke Loose*, 1605.[93] This is such a fine satire that it will be briefly discussed.

[91] Bulwer-Lytton's *Rienzi* also has a good portrait of the lack of understanding in artisans. Rienzi, the Roman tribune, in improving the condition of the commons, gathers several supporters of the craftsmen, led by a blacksmith, Cecco del Vecchio. They withdraw their support from Rienzi as soon as he is no longer able to furnish them with pageants, shows, and holidays. As in *Coriolanus* and *Julius Caesar*, ceremony and form are loved by artisans; e. g., Cecco becomes a confirmed enemy of Rienzi because the latter in a procession has not bowed to the blacksmith who stood among those looking on.

Book 9, end of chapter 1.
The disinclination of artisans to fight or to undergo sacrifices is also brought out.

F. Tupper's *Shakespearean Mob*, in "Publications of the Modern Language Association," 1912, is an excellent study of the treatment of mobs by Shakespeare and other dramatists of his period.

[92] Book 6, stanza 1.
[93] Hunterian Club ed., vol. 1.

The poem censures German Anabaptists, and typifies them in the form of various craftsmen. These wished to have plurality of wives, to govern things in their own way, and to cheat. John Leyden, a Dutch tailōr, Tom Mynter, a parish clerk, Knipperdulling, a smith, and Crafteing, a joiner, first spread these ideas:

> John Leyden, but a Taylor by his trade,
> Of Munster towne a King would needes be made:
> A Parrish Clarke, a Joyner, and a Smyth,
> His nobles were, whom hee tooke counsell with.[94]

They capture Munster, and make Leyden king. He claims that Adam, like himself, was a tailor (referring to the far-fetched story of Adam and Eve's sewing aprons of fig leaves) ; since we are all Adam's sons, we ought to be all kings, and be free from any government. His lack of direction of the uprising, and his appeal to the various craftsmen are expressed as follows:

> Let's turne the world cleane upside downe, (mad slaves)
> So to be talk'd of, when were in our graves.
>
> Brave Knipperdulling, set thy Forge on fire.
> It shall be done this present night (quoth hee,)
> Tom Mynter, leave amen unto the Quier.
> Quoth Tom, I scorne henceforth a Clarke to bee,
> Carnellis, hang thy wooden Joyners trade,
> For Noble-men apeece you shall be made.
>
> And fellowmates, nobles and Gallants all,
> To Maiestie you must your mindes dispose;
> My Lord Hans Hogg, forsake your Butchers stall.
> Hendrick the Botcher, cease from heeling Hose.

[94] Page 11.

Classe Chaundler, let your Weick and Tallow lye,
And Peeter Cobler, cast your old Shooes by.[95]

Their lack of judgment is further ridiculed in their rebellion against restrictions as to more than one wife, against taxation and penalties of any kind: Since animals and fishes do not have to pay taxes, why should man?

What reason is it when the hands have stole,
To put the Legs into a wodden hole?[96]

Thinking that they shall have permanent possession of Munster, they ring bells, *For joy a Taylor is become a King.* Leyden commands the poorer craftsmen, such as joiners and smiths, to force the rich merchants, mercers, and goldsmiths, to supply them gratis with silks, jewelry, and rich food. Their grand state does not last long, however, for they are soon besieged by the Duke of Saxony. They are then compelled to eat old shoes, chandlers' and scriveners' old wares to prevent themselves from starving. Leyden, loving the theatrical and spectacular, sends his wife to play the part of Judith and save them. The rebels are finally captured, tortured, and executed.

The satire succeeds well in ridiculing a blind and unorganized artisan uprising, the love of the rebels for perpetuating their names;[97] their boasting of high

[95] Pages 17 and 18.

[96] *Wodden hole,* i. e., wooden hole, the stocks.

[97] This was a characteristic of many artisans also who were not anarchists; e. g., Gresham in Heywood's *If You Know Not me, You Know Nobody,* Part 2, written in the same year as *Hells Broke Loose,* 1605.

Vanity of Vanities, 1659; and *The Lamentations of a Bad Market,* 1660, are ballads that satirize John Leyden.

lineage; their comparing themselves with kings (it is brought out in the rebels' clamors that Tamburlaine, though at first only a shepherd, became king); and their love of the theatrical and spectacular.

A play somewhat late for our study is interesting partly because of its own merits and partly because of its reflection on contemporary politics. Tatham's *The Rump*, 1660,[98] represents apprentices as rowdies who claim considerable rights in the government. They threaten dire revenge on Hewson, a one-eyed shoe-maker who had risen to rank under Cromwell, and demand a free parliament. Their derision of Hewson, whom they pelt with turnips, is expressed as follows:

FIRST.   He has spun a fine thread to-day.
SECOND. It may bring him to his end.
FIRST.   St. Hugh's bones must go to the rack and there let him take his last, — Whoop, Cobler![99]

In the fifth act[100] apprentices, whooping as usual, enter with faggots on their shoulders and rumps of mutton on spits. "Roast the rump" is their cry: they are about to make a public ceremony that represents the destruction of the Rump Parliament. On wood which is painted like a pile of faggots they turn and roast a rump of mutton, carousing and drinking in the meantime.[101]

The play ends in a victory for the Royalists, and disparagement of Mrs. Cromwell and Hewson. The

[98] J. Maidment and W. H. Logan edition of 1879.
[99] Act 4, sc. 1.
[100] Act 5, p. 269.
[101] According to Pepys' *Diary*, vol. 1, page 24, rumps of mutton were actually burned at this time by butchers in the Strand.

discomfited Hewson is represented as speaking the following words:

Have you any old boots or shoes to mend? I have helpt to underlay the Government this twenty years, and have been upon the mending hand, but I fear now I shall be brought to my last, and therefore ought to mind my end.[102]

Although artisans liked to imitate the courtly classes and to intermarry with the nobility, the two classes hated one another. The rivalry between gallants and artisans is a favorite theme with the writers on city life; e. g., Middleton in his *Michaelmas Term*. The gentry had from early times scorned craftsmen and traders, had used the terms, "tailor," "cobbler," "collier," "base cogging merchant," etc., as synonyms of disgust, although they depended on these substantial workers for their existence. The craftsmen, in turn, swindled the gallants, and resorted to usury whenever such practices were possible.[103] Several plays represent well the hatred between the self-made man and the man of high blood. In *Arden of Feversham*, 1592, Mosbie, the despised tailor, kills the rich Arden with the pressing iron that Arden had belittled as the stamp of the tailor's craft. In *Histriomastix*, 1599, the dependence of the higher classes on tradesmen is stressed. Massinger's *New Way to Pay Old Debts*, 1632, is one of the best works to show the growing hatred between the two classes.

[102] Act 5, p. 276. Note the frequency of terms like "mend," "end," and "last," which are technicalities of the shoemakers' craft.
Ballads that satirize Hewson are *A Hymn to the Gentle Craft*, 1659; *The Gang*, 1659; and *The Traitor's Downfall*, 1660.
[103] Plays that represent to a certain extent this mutual hatred and relation between the gentry and the artisan class are Shirley and Chapman's *The Ball*, 1632, and Shirley's *Gamester*, 1637.

One result of the Puritan Revolution was the elevation of people of low rank to positions of eminence. Cromwell, a brewer's son, advanced himself and others.

> He soon forsook the Dray and Sling, and
> Counted a Brew-house a petty thing,
> Unto the stately Throne of a King...
> It far surpast a Tun.[104]

As his wife says of him, "he could give titles of honor to the meanest peasants — made brewers, draymen, coblers, tinkers, or anybody, lords."[105] Besides Cromwell himself, others of low rank are Woodfleet, son of a custard maker, one of the competitors after Cromwell's death for the Protectorship; and Hewson, a one-eyed shoemaker, who becomes eminent in Cromwell's service. The Puritan Revolution was, then, social and industrial as well as religious and political.

With the advent of the Cavaliers, ridicule of the craftsmen and Puritans increased. The Puritans were usually of the middle class, and often represented some trade. Something may be said, before closing this chapter, of the attitude of dramatists toward Puritans.[106] Actors and dramatists naturally hated Puritans and ridiculed them at every opportunity, because these sought the suppression of plays. As early as 1601, Sir Toby Belch, in Shakespeare's *Twelfth Night*, says to the austere steward, Malvolio:

> Dost thou think, because thou art virtuous, there shall be no more cakes and ale?[107]

[104] From the ballad, *The Traitor's Downfall*, Roxburghe Ballad Socy., vol. 7, p. 660.
Another ballad that satirizes Cromwell and his family is *Joan's Ale was new.*
[105] *The Rump*, Act 5, sc. 1.
[106] This study will, of course, be restricted to the Puritans who represent trades.
[107] Act 2, sc. 3.

The others express their disgust at Malvolio's interference with their revelry, several of them calling him
a Puritan. In a number of plays Puritans are introduced as victims of satire. Thus, Chapman's *An Humorous Day's Mirth*, 1599, pictures Florila, a Puritan
wife of an old husband. *The Puritan*, published in
1607,[108] is a satire on the middle class, and on Puritans.
In Thomas Killigrew's *Parson's Wedding*, 1640, Crop,
a scrivener and Brownist,[109] is a figure that receives
attention.

In Mayne's *City Match*, c. 1639, and in Middleton's
Family of Love, printed in 1608, are more intimate
associations of Puritans with crafts. In the former, a
sempstress is spoken of as being a Puritan at her
needle; i. e., she sews religious designs in petticoats,
as was the custom of Puritans then.[110] In *The Family
of Love*, Puritan extremists are satirized, especially in
the person of an apothecary's wife.

The most interesting feature of Puritans in this
study is in their stubborn opposition to plays or fairs.
Several amusing characters of this type are Hob, in
Fletcher's *Women Pleased;* Oliver, in Middleton's
Mayor of Queenborough; and Busy, in Jonson's *Bar-
tholomew Fair*.

In *The Mayor of Queenborough*, 1596, Simon, a tanner, and Oliver, a Puritan and fustian-weaver, are
candidates for the mayoralty. Oliver was also twice
ale-conner; i. e., an officer who keeps account of ale.

[108] It has the initials, "W. S.", and was hence erroneously
thought to be by Shakespeare. The play is in C. F. T. Brooke's
Shakespeare Apocrypha.
[109] Brownism was a theory of church government named after
the sixteenth century Puritan, Robert Browne, who introduced it.
[110] Act 2, sc. 2.

Simon is chosen mayor, to the chagrin of Oliver. The latter, a so-called Puritan rebel, is captured and ridiculed by his captors in their presentation of a play.

> .... the only way
> To execute a Puritan, is seeing of a play.[111]

The Puritans themselves, however, were frequently engaged in these very crafts that catered to vanity, and this fact furnishes the theme for an excellent satire on Puritans; i. e., Thomas Randolph's *Muse's Looking-Glass*, 1638.[112] The scene is in the neighborhood of Black-Fryars, which was noted for Puritans and feathermakers and for a combination of both. There are two Puritans: Bird, a featherman, with feathers for the play-house; and Mrs. Flowerdew, wife to a haberdasher of small wares, with pins and looking-glasses. Talking of the corruption of the times, they criticize the play before they see it. Bird, who has a somewhat guilty conscience in spite of his prudery, says that such performances often ridicule persons who try to sell false wares. They scold Roscius, the player, because of his vain profession; but he, in turn, points out that both of them have crafts that wait on vanity: pins for laces, ruffs, etc., and feathers which give wing to pride.

These Puritans are finally persuaded to see the play, which is called *The Muse's Looking-Glass*. Afraid of being corrupted by even looking at it, they criticize it throughout the whole performance. Roscius says that this performance cures beholders of sin and ignorance, a statement which reconciles the Puritans to an extent.

[111] Act 5, sc. 1.
[112] Dodsley's *Old English Plays*, vol. 9.

Neither in this chapter nor in the preceding ones have all the works introducing artisans been mentioned. In many works these characters are so poorly delineated that little would be gained by discussing them. The repetitious feature of many works is also obvious: the heroic apprentice is a theme treated in many works in prose, verse (including ballad), and drama; cheating of craftsmen is treated also in these different forms of literature. Some miscellaneous works, though not mentioned as yet, are of some general interest. There are humorous domestic ballads that hardly contribute anything directly to this study, but that are of some interest to the general reader. One of the most interesting of domestic ballads touching on crafts is *The Industrious Smith*.[113] This poem is very vivid in its description of an alehouse. It tells of a smith who becomes poor and asks his wife to help him by selling ale. She consenting, they get a girl, Besse, to welcome the guests. Very noisy customers frequent the place thereafter; these flirt with the smith's wife and maid, and refuse to pay their bills. The wife answers the smith's remonstrance in every case by the following words which form the humorous refrain of the ballad:

These things must be if we sell ale.

Other ballads dealing with drunkenness are *The Jovial Tinker, The Drunken Butcher of Tideswell,* and *Half a dozen good Wives. The Cooper of Norfolke, The*

---

[113] Roxburghe Ballads, vol. 2, p. 94.

Romantic rather than realistic ballads are *The Merry Pranks of Robin Goodfellow, The Devonshire Nymph, True Love Exalted,* and Deloney's *Patient Grissel.*

Cobbler of Colchester, and *The Pinnyng of the Basket* are equally interesting.

Certain late ballads in D'Urfey's *Pills to Purge Melancholy* describe craftsmen in detail, often introducing vulgar or obscene associations with work or tools. Satirical and unpleasant works not restricted to crafts are certain versified portrayals of social climbers, their intermarriages with those of higher rank, and the consequent degradation of society. Instances are *Cornu-copiae, Pasquils Nightcap,*[114] printed in 1612; and *Pasquils Palinodia,* 1619.[115] Ballads with somewhat similar themes are *The Jolly Miller, The London Prentice, The Country Wake,* and *The Lamentation of an ale Wifes Daughter.*

Interesting prose works that introduce craftsmen among other individuals and that contain much satire and punning on the technical terms of the craft are the Character books.[116] They repeat much that has already been given in this chapter, presenting among other persons citizens and artisans who defraud customers and who aspire to nobility. Elizabethan imitations of Chaucer's works and some of Dekker's poems, one on a merchant, the other on an artificer, in his *Papist Encountred,* 1606, show an approximation to this type. Some instances in prose are John Stephen's *Essayes and Characters,* 1615, in which are delineated among others a tapster and a tailor's man; John Taylor's *An Armado,* 1627, in which the state of apprenticeship is gently satirized, his *A Bawd,* 1635 (partly

---

[114] Grosart's *Occasional Issues,* vol. 5.
[115] Grosart's *Occasional Issues,* vol. 5.
[116] Collections of these works are J. O. Halliwell's *Books of Characters* and H. Morley's *Character Writings of the 17th Century.*

verse), in which four of the greatest livery companies, the mercers, grocers, fishmongers, and goldsmiths are subjected to uncomplimentary comparisons; Don Lupton's *London and the Country Carbonadoed and Quartered into severall Characters*, 1632, which stresses the courtesy of alewives and the dishonesty of goldsmiths; *Whimzies*, 1631, in which painters, peddlers, newspaper writers, launderers, almanac-makers, and exchange-men are held up to ridicule, attention being given to the psychology of advertising; Sir Thomas Overbury's *Characters*, 1614, in which a tailor, a tinker, an almanac-maker, a quack-salver, and a French cook are described; Nicholas Breton's *Good and Bad*, 1616, in which are contrasted a good and a bad merchant; John Earle's *Micro-Cosmographie*, 1628, in which are described bakers, cooks, shopkeepers, citizens, and aldermen. *The Wandering Jew telling Fortunes to Englishmen*, 1649, is a rather unique work that presents among others a cobbler, an alderman's supercilious son, a citizen's fashion-loving wife and an apprentice, the youngest son of a gentleman, all desirous of knowing their fortune, as are the patronizers of Alice West. In this work the various eccentricities and desires of the inquirers are exposed.

CONCLUSION

Twentieth century readers, as well as students of the Middle Ages and Elizabethan period, may be interested in the preceding study of the medieval and Elizabethan craftsman in literature.

Modern writers, such as Carlyle, Ruskin, Morris, Whittier, Longfellow, Rolland, Hauptmann, Ibsen, D'Annunzio, and Guiterman revert at times to the master-craftsman and his artistry, or to the medieval guild system, with its original emphasis on co-operation, brotherhood, and equality.

Persistence even to the present day of a theory somewhat like that of the guild may be seen in the fact that the place formerly occupied by the latter is now occupied, to a certain extent, by the Trade Unions, the Mechanics' Association of American cities, the Masonic Order, and Guild Socialism.

Medieval and Elizabethan apprenticeship, though not at any time a perfect system, was a far better method of education for young persons than many of the later forms; e. g., the rigid factory system of the 18th and 19th centuries.

To the modern reader one of the most interesting aspects of this study is found in the treatment of the self-made man, whose rise to prominence presents a few parallels to the typical self-made man of more recent date. Although the stories of Whittington, Eyre, and Thornton are apparently exaggerated accounts of the fulfillment of seemingly idle dreams, such narratives are possible. What could be more illustrative poetically of the speculating and commercial Elizabethan age than Whittington's dream and its fulfillment as described in the ballad? What, moreover, could be more illustrative of the great age of inventions, the 19th and 20th centuries? How could we have the five and ten cent store, the cheap automobile, or the aeroplane, were it not for such dreamers as the Woolworths, Henry Ford, Langley, and the Wright brothers? The story of *Aladdin and the Wonderful Lamp* and that of *Old Fortunatus*, with all their wealth of romance and oriental splendor, are not more interesting, and are far less significant than the story of Sir Richard Whittington, who, according to popular tradition, through the original venture of a cat, became a great speculator, philanthropist, and mayor, celebrated in prose, ballad, drama and pageant.

BIBLIOGRAPHY

CATALOGUES AND DICTIONARIES

ADAMS, W. D. Dictionary of the Drama, 2 vols. London, 1904.

ADAMS, W. D. Dictionary of English Literature. London and N. Y., Cassell, Petter, and Galpin, 1878.

ARBER, E. A Transcript of the Stationers' Register. 5 vols. Privately printed, 1875-94.

ASHMOLE, E. Descriptive Catalogue of Works given to Oxford by Ashmole. Oxford University Press, 1845.

DISSERTATIONS. Alphabetized lists from Harvard, Yale, Columbia, Chicago, etc.

GRANT, COLONEL F. Catalogue of Collections of Broadsides. London, 1900.

GREEN, E. Catalogue of Somerset Chapbooks. 3 vols. Taunton, Barncott and Pearce, 1902.

HALLIWELL, J. O. Catalogue of Chapbooks, Garlands, and Histories. London, 1849.

HALLIWELL, J. O. Catalogue of Unique Collections of Ancient English Broadside Ballads. London, 1856.

HALLIWELL, J. O. Dictionary of Old English Plays. London, J. R. Smith, 1860.

Harvard Catalogue of English and American Chapbooks and Broadside Ballads in Harvard College Library. Cambridge, Library of Harvard University, 1905.

HAZLITT, W. C. Catalogue of Early English Miscellanies formerly in Harleian Library. Camden Socy., vol. 87. London, 1862.

HAZLITT, W. C. Handbook to Popular, Poetic, and Dramatic Literature. London, J. R. Smith, 1867.

HENSLOW, P. Diary. Edited by W. Greg. 2 vols. London, A. H. Bullen, 1904-8.

151

Jahres-Verzeichniss der an den Deutschen Universitaten erschienen Schriften. 35 vols. Berlin, 1887-1920.

LEMON, R.   Catalogue of a Collection of Printed Broadsides of the Society of Antiquaries. London, 1866.

Library of Congress.   A List of American Doctoral Dissertations, 1912-1920.   9 vols. Government Printing Office, Washington.

LOWNDES, W. T.   Bibliographers' Manual. 4 vols. London, W. Pickering, 1834.

LUDOVIC, EARL OF CRAWFORD.   Bibliotheca Lindesiana. London, B. Quaritch, 1884.

NEWTON, T. W.   Catalogue of Old Ballads, now at Haigh Hall. London, privately printed for T. Scott, 1877.

OUVRY, F.   Catalogue of Ballads of F. Ouvry. London, privately printed by T. Scott, 1877.

COLLECTIONS

ASHTON, J.   A Century of Ballads. London, Stock, 1887.

ASHTON, J.   Modern Street Ballads. London, 1888.

BAGFORD, J.   Amanda Group of Bagford Ballads. Hertford, 1880.

BAGFORD, J.   Bagford Ballads. 3 vols. Hertford, 1877-8.

BATES, L.   Ballad Book. Boston, 1890.

BELL, R.   Early Ballads. London, 1856.

BELOE, W.   Anecdotes of Literature and Scarce Books. 6 vols. London, 1808-14.

A Collection of Ballads including English Caricatures. Preston (18-).

A Collection of Chapbooks. Glasgow, 1818-60.

COLLIER, J. P.   Bibliographical and Critical Accounts of the Rarest Books. 4 vols. New York, 1866.

COLLIER, J. P.   Book of Roxburghe Ballads. London, 1842.

COLLIER, J. P.   Broadsides and Blackletter Ballads in the 16th and 17th centuries. London, 1868.

COLLIER, J. P.   Broadsides of Speeches and Songs. London, 1863.

COLLIER, J. P. Illustrations of Early English Popular Literature. 2 vols. London, 1863-4.

COLLIER, J. P. Miscellaneous Tracts. 15 nos. in 5 vols. London, 1870.

COLLIER, J. P. Old Ballads. London, printed for Percy Socy., 1840.

DODSLEY, R. Old English Plays. 15 vols. Revised by W. C. Hazlitt. London, 1874-6.

D'URFEY, T. Wit and Mirth. 6 vols. London, 1719-20.

English Broadside Ballads. London, 1856. Given to Glasgow University Library.

EVANS, T. Old Ballads. 4 vols. London, 1810.

FAIRHOLT, F. W. Lord Mayors' Pageants. Percy Socy., vol. 10.

FURNIVALL, F. J. Ballads from Manuscripts. 2 vols. London, printed for Ballad Socy., 1868-73.

GREENE, R. Works, A. B. Grosart. 15 vols. London, 1881-86.

GROSART, A. B. Occasional Issues. 17 vols. Privately printed for subscribers, 1875.

HALLIWELL, J. O. Contributions to Early English Literature of the 16th and 17th Centuries. London, 1849.

HALLIWELL, J. O. Descriptive Notices of Popular English Histories. London, printed for Percy Socy., 1849.

HALLIWELL, J. O. Early English Miscellanies. London, 1855.

HARLAND, J. Ballads and Songs of Lancashire. London, Routledge, 1875.

Harleian Miscellany. 12 vols. London, 1808-11.

HART, W. M. English Popular Ballads. Chicago and New York, Scott, Foresman and Co., 1916.

HAZLITT, W. C. Jest-Books. 3 vols. London, Willis, 1864.

HINDLEY, C. Old Book Collectors' Miscellany. vol. 1, Ballads. London, Reeves and Turner, 1871-73. 3 vols.

JONSON, B. Works. Ed. by P. Whalley. 7 vols. London, 1756.

KINARD, J. P. Old English Ballads. New York, 1902.

LILLY, J. A Collection of Seventy-nine Blackletter Ballads and

Broadsides printed in the Reign of Queen Elizabeth, 1559-1597. London, J. Lilly, 1867.

MACKAY, C. A Collection of Songs and Ballads relative to the London Apprentices and Trades. Percy Socy., vol 1.

MORFILL, W. R. Ballads from Manuscripts. 2 vols. London, printed for Ballad Socy., 1868-73.

MORLEY, H. Character Writings of the 17th Century. London, 1891.

New Shakespeare Society Publications. 8 series. London, 1874-84.

OLIPHANT, T. Collection of Old Songs, mainly Elizabethan. London, 1837.

Percy Society Publications. 30 vols. London, 1840-52.

PHILIPS, A. Collection of Old Ballads. 3 vols. London, 1723-25.

RITSON, J. Northern Garlands. London, 1810.

RITSON, J. Pieces of Ancient Popular Poetry. London, 1833.

ROWLANDS, S. The Complete Works of Samuel Rowlands. Glasgow, printed for Hunterian Club, 1880.

Roxburghe Ballads. Ed. by C. Hindley. 2 vols. London, Reeves and Turner, 1873-74.

Roxburghe Ballads. 9 vols. London, printed for the Ballad Socy., 1874-99.

Shakespeare Jahrbuch. 57 vols. Berlin, 1865-1915.

Shakespeare Society Publications. 20 vols. London, 1841-51.

Shirburn Ballads. Oxford, 1907.

Spenser Society Publications. 55 vols. in 51. Manchester, 1867-88; 1889-95.

HISTORIES

BESANT, SIR W. London in the Time of the Stuarts. **London, A. and C. Black, 1903.**

BESANT, SIR W. London in the Time of the Tudors. **London, A. and C. Black, 1904.**

BESANT, SIR W. Sir Richard Whittington, Lord Mayor of London. **New York, G. P. Putnam and Sons, 1881.**

BRENTANO, L. English Guilds. London, published for Early English Text Society by N. Trübner and Co., 1870.

BRODSKY, R. Das Lehrlingswesen in England in 15 und 16 Jahrhundert. Heidelberg, J. Hornig, 1907.

BUDIG, W. Untersuchungen über Jane Shore. A Thesis, Rostock. Schwerin i. M. 1908.

CHAPPELL, W. Popular Music of Old Times. 2 vols. London, 1859.

CLODE, C. M. Guild of the Merchant-Taylors. London, Harrison and Sons, 1875.

DASENT, J. R. Acts of the Privy Council. Vols. 1-32. London, 1890-1907.

DUNLOP, O. J. and DENMAN, R. D. English Apprenticeship and Child Labor. New York, Macmillan, 1912.

GARDINER, S. R. History of England from the Accession of James I to the Outbreak of the Civil War, 1603-1642. 10 vols. London. N. Y., Longmans, Green and Co., 1893-5.

GRAFTON, R. Chronicle. 2 vols. London, 1809.

GROSS, C. The Gild Merchant. 2 vols. Oxford, Clarendon Press, 1890.

HALL, H. Society in the Elizabethan Age. London, 1886.

HAYES, C. J. H. A Political and Social History of Modern Europe. 2 vols. N. Y., Macmillan Co., 1916-18.

HAZLITT, W. C. Livery Companies of London. Their origin. London, 1892.

HERBERT, W. The History of the Twelve Great Livery Companies of London. 2 vols. London, published by the author, 1837.

HINDLEY, C. History of the Cries of London. London, 1884.

KRAMER, S. English Craft Guilds. New York, 1905.

LIPSON, E. An Introduction to the Economic History of England. London, Black, 1915.

RENARD, G. F. Guilds in the Middle Ages. Translated by D. Terry. London, 1919.

SCHELLING, F. E. Elizabethan Drama. 2 vols. Boston and N. Y., Houghton, Mifflin and Co., 1908.

STOWE, J. A Survey of London. 2 vols., C. L. Kingsford edition. Oxford, Clarendon Press, 1908.

STRYPE, J. Complete History of England. 3 vols. London, printed for B. Aylmer, 1706.

TRAILL, H. D. Social England. 6 vols. London and N. Y., Cassell and Co., limited, 1909.

UNWIN, G. Gilds and Companies of London. London, Methuen and Co., 1908.

UNWIN, G. Industrial Organization in the 16th and 17th Centuries. Oxford, at Clarendon Press, 1904.

WITHINGTON, R. English Pageantry. 2 vols. Cambridge, Harvard University Press, 1918-20.

WRIOTHESLEY, C. Chronicle of England during the Reigns of the Tudors. Ed. by W. D, Hamilton. London, 1875-77. Camden Socy. Pub., new series, vols. 11-20.

TEXTS

An Arte whose end was never knowne. Shirburn Ballads. Appendix IV.

Arden of Feversham, 1592. Edited by A. F. Hopkinson. London, 1898.

ARMIN, R. The Italian Taylor and his Boy, 1609. Grosart's Occasional Issues, vol. 14.

BAS, W. Sword and Buckler, or The Servingman's Defence, 1602. Collier's Illustrations of Early English Popular Literature, vol. 2.

BEAUMONT and FLETCHER. Knight of the Burning Pestle, 1613. Ed. by H. S. Murch. New York, 1908.

BRATHWAITE, R. To all true-bred Northern Sparks, of the generous society of the Cottoneers. In his Strappado for the Devil, 1615. Boston, 1878.

The Brewers' Plea. Printed 1647. Harleian Miscellany, vol. 7, p. 329.

BREWER, A. The Love-Sick King, 1605. Edited by A. E. H. Swaen. Louvain, A. Uystpruyst, 1907.

BROME, R. The New Academy, 1658. Dramatic Works. London, 1873, vol. 2.

The First Part of the Contention of the two famous Houses of Yorke and Lancaster, 1590. Facsimile Text.

COOKE, J. Greenes tu quoque, 1614. Dodsley's Old English Plays, vol. 7.

Cornu-copiæ, Pasquils Nightcap, 1612. Grosart's Occasional Issues, vol. 5.

CROSSE, H. Vertues Commonwealth, 1603. In Grosart's Occasional Issues, vol. 7.

DEKKER, T. Dramatic Works. 4 vols. London, 1873.

DEKKER, T. Non-dramatic Works. Ed. by A. B. Grosart. 5 vols. London, 1884-6.

DEKKER, T. Some of his pageants are in Fairholt's Lord Mayors' Pageants. Percy Socy., vol. 10.

DELONEY, T. The Gentle Craft. Edited by A. F. Lange, Ph. D. Berlin, 1903.

DELONEY, T. The Works of Thomas Deloney. Edited by F. O. Mann. Oxford, Clarendon Press, 1912.

DRAYTON, M. Edward IV to Jane Shore. In England's Heroical Epistles, 1597. London, 1695.

EARLE, J. Micro-Cosmographie, 1628. In Arber's English Reprints, vols. 10-12.

EDWARDS, R. Damon and Pithias, 1571. In Dodsley's Old English Plays, vol. 1.

F. T. Debate between Pride and Lowliness. Ed. by J. Charwood. London, 1841.

Faire Em, the Miller's Daughter of Manchester, 1587. Amersham, England. Issued for subscribers by J. S. Farmer, 1913.

FLETCHER, J. and ROWLEY, W. The Maid in the Mill, 1623. In The Works of Beaumont and Fletcher. Edited by H. Weber. 14 vols. Edin., 1812, vol. 14.

FLETCHER, J. Rollo, 1624. In Works of Beaumont and Fletcher. 1750 ed., vol. 5.

FORD, J. Perkin Warbeck, 1634. Ed. by J. P. Pickburn and J. L. Brereton. Sydney, 1896.

GASCOIGNE, G. The Steel Glas, 1576. Ed. by W. C. Hazlitt. Vol. 2, pp. 211, 212.

GREENE, R. Defence of Connycatching, 1592. Edited by A. B. Grosart. Vol. 11.

GREENE, R. A Notable Discovery of Coosnage, 1591-2. Edited by A. B. Grosart. Vol. 10.

GREENE, R. A Quip for an Upstart Courtier, 1592. In J. P. Collier's Miscellaneous Tracts. London, reprinted 1870.

Grim the Collier of Croydon, 1600 c. In Dodsley's Old English Plays, vol. 11.

GUILPIN, E. Skialetheia. In Collier's Miscellaneous Tracts, vols. 1-4.

HAKE, E. Newes out of Powles Churchyarde, 1579. In Isham Reprints, no. 2, satire 4.

HEYWOOD, T. Edward IV, 1600. 2 parts. In 1874 edition of Heywood's Works, vol. 1, and in Shakespeare Socy., vol. 5.

HEYWOOD, T. (?) Faire Maid of the Exchange, 1607. In Heywood's Dramatic Works, 1874 ed., vol. 2.

HEYWOOD, T. Faire Maid of the West, 1621 c. In Heywood's Dramatic Works, 1874 ed., vol. 2.

HEYWOOD, T. Four Prentices of London, 1594 c. In Dodsley's Old English Plays, vol. 6.

HEYWOOD, T. If You Know Not Me You Know Nobody, 1606. 2 parts. In Shakespeare Socy., vol. 6.

History of Sir Richard Whittington's Advancement. In Percy Socy., vol. 1, p. 4.

Honor of a London Prentice. In Evans' Old Ballads, vol. 3, p. 35.

JOHNSON, R. Nine Worthies of London, 1592. In Harleian Miscellany, vol. 8.

JOHNSON, R. Pleasant Walkes of Moore-Fields, 1607. In Collier's Illustrations of Early English Popular Literature, vol. 2.

JONSON, B. Bartholomew Fair. Ed. by C. S. Alden. N. Y., 1904.

JONSON, B. New Inn, 1629. Edited by G. B. Tennant. N. Y., 1908.

JONSON, B. Staple of News, 1625. In The Works of Ben Jonson, 1875 ed., vol. 5.

JONSON, B. Tale of a Tub, 1633. Ed. by F. M. Snell. London, 1915.

Kinge Edward IV and a Tanner of Tamworth, 1600. 2 parts. Roxburghe Ballads, vol. 2, p. 163.

King James I and the Tinker. In Percy Socy., vol. 17, p. 109.

Life and Death of Jack Straw, 1593. In Dodsley's Old English Plays, vol. 5.

LODGE, T. Life and Death of William Longbeard. In Lodge's Complete Works, Hunterian Club. 4 vols. Glasgow, 1883, vol. 2, p. 26.

The London Chaunticleers, 1636. In Hazlitt-Dodsley's Old English Plays, vol. 12.

Long Meg of Westminster, 1635. In Miscellanea Antiqua Anglicana.

A Looking-Glass of the World, 1644. In H. Huth's Fugitive Tracts, series 2.

MARMION, S. The Antiquary, 1641. In Hazlitt-Dodsley's Old English Plays, vol. 13.

MARMION, S. Fine Companion, 1633. In T. White's Old English Drama, 1830, vol. 4.

MARSTON, J. Works. Ed. by J. O. Halliwell. 3 vols. London, 1856.

MARSTON, J. The Dutch Courtesan, 1605. In Bullen's 3-vol. ed. of Marston's works, vol. 1.

MARSTON, J. Chapman, and Jonson's Eastward Hoe, 1605. In vol. 1 of The Works of George Chapman. London, 1874-75. 3 vols.

MARSTON, J. (?) Histriomastix, 1599. In R. Simpson's School of Shakespeare, vol. 2.

MASSINGER, P. The City Madam, 1632. In The Plays of Philip Massinger. London, 1830-31, vol. 2.

MAYNE, J.   The City Match.   In Dodsley's Old English Plays, vol. 9.

MIDDLETON, T.   Anything for a Quiet Life.   In vol. 5 of A. H. Bullen's ed. of Middleton's Works.   8 vols.   London, 1885-86, vol. 5.

MIDDLETON, T.   A Chaste Maid in Cheapside, 1630.   In vol. 5 of Bullen's edition of Middleton's Works.

MIDDLETON, T.   Michaelmas Term, 1607.   In vol. 1 of A. Dyce's edition of Middleton's Works.   5 vols.   London, 1840.

Mock-Majesty.   In Harleian Miscellany, vol. 8, p. 258.

NABBES, T.   Covent Garden, 1632.   London, 1638.

NABBES, T.   Microcosmus, 1637.   In Dodsley's Old English Plays, vol. 9.

NABBES, T.   Totenham Court, 1638.   London, 1638.

NASH, T.   Complete Works.   Ed. by A. B. Grosart.   London, 1883-85.

NASH, T.   Christ's Tears over Jerusalem, 1593.   R. B. McKerrow's ed., vol. 1, p. 135.

NASH, T.   Pierce Pennilesse, 1592.   J. P. Collier's ed., p. 2.

A New Merry Newes, 1606.   In H. Huth's Fugitive Tracts, series 2.

Pasquils Palinodia, 1619.   In Grosart's Occasional Issues, vol. 5.

Pimlyco, or Runne Red-Cap, 1609.   In Antient Drolleries, no. 2.

The Pinner of Wakefield.   In vol. 2 of The Plays and Poems of Robert Greene, edited by J. C. Collins.   Oxford, Clarendon Press, 1905.

The Pleasant Conceites of Old Hobson, 1607.   Percy Socy., vol. 9.

A Pleasant New Ballad of the Bloody Murther of Sir John Barley-Corn.   In Jamieson's Popular Ballads and Songs, vol. 2, p. 251.

POWELL, T.   Tom of All Trades, 1631.   In New Shakespeare Socy., series 6, 2.

RANDOLPH, T.   The Muses Looking-Glass, 1638.   In Dodsley's Old English Plays, vol. 9.

RAWLINS, T.   The Rebellion, 1637.   In Hazlitt-Dodsley's Old English Plays, vol. 14.

RICH, B. The Honesty of this Age, 1614. In Percy Socy., vol. 11.

RICKETS, J. Byrsa Basilica, 1570. In Jahrbuch der Deutschen Shakespeare Gesellschaft, vol. 34, p. 281.

ROBERTS, H. Fame's Trumpet, 1589. In H. Huth's Fugitive Tracts, Series 1.

ROBERTS, H. Haigh for Devonshire, 1600. In the February, 1885, issue of the Western Antiquary is an account by W. B. Rye of this plagiarism of Thomas of Reading.

ROWLANDS, S. Doctor Merrie-Man, 1609. In Hunterian Club ed. of Rowlands' works, vol. 2, pp. 11, 12.

ROWLANDS, S. Good News and Bad News, 1622. In Hunterian Club, vol. 2.

ROWLANDS, S. Hells Broke Loose, 1605. In Hunterian Club, vol. 1.

ROWLANDS, S. The Knave of Harts. In Percy Socy., vol. 9.

ROWLANDS, S. Knaves of Spades and Diamonds. In Percy Socy., vol. 9, pp. 104 and 111.

ROWLANDS, S. A Paire of Spy-Knaves. In Hunterian Club, vol. 2.

ROWLEY, W. A New Wonder, 1632. In Hazlitt-Dodsley's Old English Plays, vol. 12.

ROWLEY, W. A. Shoemaker a Gentleman, 1609. Edited by C. W. Stork. Phil., pub. for the University, 1910.

The Plays of William Shakespeare. To which are added notes by S. Johnson and G. Steevens.

Coriolanus, 1609. Vol. 7.

Henry IV. 2 parts. 1597-9. Vol. 5.

Julius Caesar, 1599. Vol. 8.

A Midsummer Night's Dream, 1594-5. Vol. 3.

Richard II, 1595. Vol. 5.

A Winter's Tale, 1611. Vol. 4.

SHIRLEY, J. Dramatic Works with notes by W. Gifford and A. Dyce. 6 vols. London, 1833.

—Honoria and Mammon, 1639. Vol. 6.

—Hyde Park, 1632. Vol. 2.

STEPHEN, J.   Essayes and Characters, 1615. In J. O. Halliwell's Books of Characters. Character 26.

STUBBES, P.   Anatomy of Abuses, part 2, 1583. In New Shakespeare Socy., Series 6, 12.

Tarlton's Jests, Shakespeare Socy., 1920.

Tarlton's Jigge of a horse loade of Fooles (before 1588). In Shakespeare Socy., 1920.

Tarlton's Newes out of Purgatory (before 1598). In Shakespeare Socy., 1920.

TATHAM, J.   The Rump, 1660. J. Maidment and W. H. Logan ed. of 1879.

TAYLOR, J.   A Full and compleat answer against the Writer of a Tale in a Tub. In Spenser Socy., vol. 7.

— Jack a Lent. In Spenser Socy., vols. 2-4.

— Praise of Clean Linnen. In Spenser Socy., vols. 2-4.

— Praise of Hempseed. In Spenser Socy., vols. 2-4.

— Praise of the Needle. In Spenser Socy., vol. 7.

— Superbiæ Flagellum. In Spenser Socy., vols. 2-4.

— A Tale in a Tub. In Spenser Socy., vol. 7.

— Travels of Twelve-Pence. In Spenser Socy., vols. 2-4.

— The True Cause of the Watermen's Suit concerning Players. In Spenser Socy., vols. 2-4.

—The Whole Life and Progresse of Henry Walker the Ironmonger. In Spenser Socy., vol. 7.

— The World runnes on Wheels. In Spenser Socy., vols. 2-4.

Taylor's Pastorall. In Spenser Socy., vols. 2-4.

Thomas Lord Cromwell, 1602. Ed. by A. F. Hopkinson. London, 1899.

The Tinker of Turvey, 1600 c. Ed. by J. O. Halliwell. London, 1859.

Tom Tyler and his Wife. In J. S. Farmer's Six Anonymous Plays.

The Traitor's Downfall, 1660. In Roxburghe Ballad Socy., vol. 7, p. 660.

UDALL, N. Ralph Roister Doister, 1553 c. Edited by W. H. Williams and P. A. Robin. London, 1911.

A Warning for Fair Women, 1599. In R. Simpson's School of Shakespeare, vol. 2.

The Weakest Goeth to the Wall, 1600. Amersham, England. Issued for subscribers by J. S. Farmer, 1913.

Westward for Smelts, 1603 c. In Percy Socy., vol. 21.

WILSON, R. The Pedler's Prophecy. Amersham, England. Issued for subscribers by J. S. Farmer, 1913.

The Wisdom of Doctor Dodypoll, 1600. In vol. 3 of A. H. Bullen's Old Plays. 4 vols. Library of Congress, 1882.

WITHER, G. Haleluiah, 1641. Hymns 42, 53, and 54. In Spenser Socy., vol. 27.

The Woeful Lamentation of Jane Shore, a Goldsmith's Wife in London, sometime King Edward the Fourths Concubine. 2 parts. In Philips' Old Ballads, vol. 1, p. 145.

INDEX